This anthology was devised and edited by
Sherry Ashworth, Iris Feindt and Livi Michael.
Published by The Manchester Writing School
Department of English
Manchester Metropolitan University

First edition published October 2013.

Illustrations supervised and co-ordinated by
Louise Clennell, Ian McCullough and Sharon Scholey.

With thanks to Manchester Metropolitan University
Special Collections.

Designed by Jo Phillips, The Design Studio,
Marketing, Communications and Development, MMU.

A Manchester Children's Book Festival project:
www.mcbf.org.uk

Printed and bound in England by
MMU Print Services.

ISBN 978-1-905476-91-6

Time lines

tales from the past by writers of the present and future

Contents

1	David Crabtree	**Diary of a T. Rex** *Illustration: Sam Croasdale*
12	N. M. Browne	**The Betrothed** *Illustration: Sabina Drinceanu*
22	Marie Dentan	**Robin and the King** *Illustration: Stephanie Coathupe*
31	Lucinda Nettleton	**The Hunting** *Illustration: Alexandra Healey*
45	Guy Vernon	**Thomas Goodman and The Great Fire of London** *Illustration: Stephanie Shaw*
54	Jackie Goddard	**Riders' Business** *Illustration: Bethany Thompson*
65	Matt Killeen	**Lucky Hits the Skin** *Illustration: Bridget Collin*
76	Kim Hutson	**The Silver Spoons of Ordsall Hall** *Illustration: Bethany White*
87	Kat Williams	**The Passenger** *Illustration: Bethany White*

98 Paula Warrington **Thicker Than Water**
Illustration: Jennifer Quinn

109 Anna Mainwaring **Maharajah: the Elephant who Walked to Manchester**
Illustration: Nabihah Shireen

120 Sherry Ashworth **The John Library**
Illustration: Stephanie Coathupe

131 Alison Padley-Woods **The Fall**
Illustration: Harry Fryer

143 Jason E Hill **Waiting for the Kick-Off**
Illustration: Daniel Garrity

155 Emma George **The Hangman's Daughter**
Illustration: Stephanie Shaw

168 Iris Feindt **The White Line**
Illustration: Jennifer Quinn

179 Livi Michael **Key**
Illustration: Abigail Woodhouse

Diary of a T. Rex

DAVID CRABTREE

DAY ONE IN THE LATE CRETACEOUS PERIOD. Roughly sixty five million years ago. Probably about lunch time.

The first thing I thought when I arrived in the steaming jungles of the late Cretaceous period was, *Wow! The time machine really worked!* This was quickly followed by, *Wait…I'm in the Cretaceous Period. I'm going to be killed by dinosaurs!* Then finally I thought, *Why does everything feel so weird?*

So yeah, apparently time travel has some odd side effects. I felt way too heavy and stiff and my body felt like it'd been stretched and pushed into a weird new shape. I knew something had gone *very* wrong.

Normally I don't swear, but this time I let loose a real nasty one at the top of my voice…except it didn't come out as a swear word. It didn't come out as a word at all. I tried to swear, but what came out instead was a roar. A loud, bellowing roar. The jungle around me came alive as a ripple of unseen creatures scuttled away into the undergrowth. I tried to swear again, but I just roared once more.

It was then that I decided I desperately needed to find out what had happened to me. I set off into the jungle to look for a pond or a stream, basically anything to check my reflection in.

Day One, a few hours later.

I'd been walking for ages and still hadn't come across a drop of water. There were plenty of insects about, huge droning things that make modern day bugs look tiny in comparison. Still, I'd started to realise what had happened. I couldn't quite believe it, but all the clues were there. The roaring, the feeling of being way too front heavy, the way everything looked and smelled weirdly different. There was only one explanation…I was a dinosaur!

At the time, I didn't know what kind of dinosaur I was. Judging by my eye level in comparison to the trees I knew I was pretty big. When I tried to look at my hands all I managed to do was give myself aching wrists. I was a huge dinosaur with tiny, puny arms.

Walking also wasn't easy to begin with. You see humans are pretty upright (even people like me who used to slouch all the time are still pretty upright compared to most dinosaurs). It took a while to get used to my new weight distribution. I was a lot heavier at my front than my middle. Fortunately I had a tail to help me balance. I've always thought it would be cool if humans had tails. Spider monkeys have a prehensile tail. That means they can use it like an extra limb. If humans had a tail like that…I'm getting off track.

What mattered most to me at the time was finding out what kind of dinosaur I was. I carried on looking for something that might show me my reflection.

Day One, late evening.

I wandered through the jungle for God only knows how long. I kept seeing shapes flit into the trees as I approached. I was too slow to get a proper look at them and they were well camouflaged anyway.

They just disappeared into the ferns. I could smell them though. Boy, could I smell them! My vision wasn't great, but I could sniff out every living thing over a huge distance. There were *hundreds* of little creatures scampering away in every direction. I guess they could smell me, too.

As I trudged through the jungle, I caught a glimpse of something that hadn't run away from me. If I'm honest, I didn't like the thought of facing a dinosaur that wasn't scared of me. I also didn't like the prospect of being ambushed by said dinosaur, so I stopped walking and looked around. Nothing. I looked a little harder and saw a rustling in the foliage. Whatever was out there was circling me. I didn't know what to do so I stamped my feet and hissed as loudly as I could. That seemed to do the trick. Something scaly and frightened bolted out of the undergrowth and scampered away, scaring me half to death in the process. I took a moment to calm my nerves, reassured myself that I was far bigger than anything else I'd seen so far, then carried on my journey.

Now obviously I had no idea where I was going so I ended up walking in whatever direction seemed right. Eventually this tactic paid off and I came to a clearing in the trees.

Right in the centre of the clearing was a huge lake. I saw a herd of Triceratops gathered at one end of it. The younger ones huddled behind the adults when I appeared out of the trees and bleated in fear. The adults didn't seem too bothered though; aside from the odd snort and stamp of a foot I reckoned they knew I wasn't about to charge headlong into a wall of thick scales and metre long horns.

I kept my distance from the Triceratops herd and made sure I didn't look like I might try to attack their young. Being trampled to death by a group of ten tonne monsters isn't the way I want to go. I went up to the edge of the pool and looked at my reflection… the face looking back at me was a T. Rex. A bloody T. Rex, the poster-boy of the dinosaur world.

I looked again just to make sure my eyes weren't playing tricks on me. Nope, definitely a T. Rex – dagger long teeth and all. That was when I really thought about it properly for the first time. I was a dinosaur! Not just any dinosaur either, I was a Tyrannosaurus Rex, the king of the dinosaur world. Me. A T. Rex. Have you ever had one of those dreams where you suddenly realise you have superpowers? I kind of felt like that. I roared at the sky. All around me creatures panicked and fled into the undergrowth. Even the Triceratops herd backed away warily. Understand that this time I wasn't roaring because I wanted to swear but couldn't form the words. This time I was roaring because *I was a T. Rex!*

Day Two, early morning

I'd spent the rest of my first night as a dinosaur stomping around and roaring, crashing through the jungle and watching the smaller dinosaurs scatter in fear. It's an amazing feeling, like somebody's just taken away all the responsibility and rules in life and let you run free. I basically kept on running, smashing through trees and bellowing until I'd exhausted myself to sleep.

I woke up next to a giant rock formation. The shade it gave me had vanished and the sun glared down at me from above. I guess if I'd had human flesh the sun would be unbearable. As it was, I just didn't care. Even the biggest dinosaurs would think twice about disturbing a sleeping T. Rex and the sun was pleasantly warm on my scales.

It was at this moment that I realised the downside to being a gigantic carnivore with teeth the size of daggers. As I woke up and

staggered to my feet, hunger set in. This wasn't just like being a bit peckish either. It was a gnawing animal hunger that ached right down to my core. I took a few gulps of water from a nearby pool to take the edge off (not an easy task by the way and it took me a few tries before I managed to stop most of it spilling straight back out of my mouth). Once I'd had a few mouthfuls of water I set off to find something to eat.

The Triceratops were off the menu straight away. No way was I going to try and take them on, in fact I wasn't keen on the idea of trying to fight any dinosaur I couldn't swallow in one mouthful. Also, most of the creatures I could smell were too small and skittish. Any time I turned to face one I'd just catch a glimpse of a tail disappearing into the undergrowth. That left only one option and it wasn't a pleasant one either.

Amidst the countless odours coming off the small dinosaurs nearby I could detect another, stronger smell. It was a powerful stench, a lot like rancid chicken, except as a T. Rex I could smell it a lot more keenly than I'd have been able to as a human. Also, while I'd have been close to puking as a human, this smelled weirdly tasty.

Day Two, noon.

I discovered fairly quickly just how powerful my sense of smell was. Whatever I'd caught the scent of was a long way away. Well actually it was probably about half a mile away all in all, but getting to the source was tough. I had to navigate my way through thick jungle, trying to stay focussed on the one scent and not be distracted by the thousands of others surrounding me. The little squirrel-like creatures in particular seemed quite tasty and it took all my willpower not to chase after them and snatch them up.

I let my nose lead me through the jungle until I finally found what I was looking for. Lying only a few feet in front of me was the carcass of an Edmontosaurus (which look something like a twelve metre long hybrid between an iguana and a cow). It was pretty ripe, with ribs sticking through its skin and a huge cloud of flies hovering over it. Even though I was a T. Rex, the human side of my mind was grossed out at the thought of eating a dead dinosaur. Still, the hunger was actually physically painful by that point. I leaned down and took a bite.

I can't describe how good it felt to eat that rancid carcass! If I'd been human I'd have been retching between every mouthful, but as a T. Rex it was like sitting down to a banquet at a classy restaurant. My first bite had been small, just to test the water so to speak, but after that I started gorging myself. I tore into the Edmontosaurus as though I hadn't eaten in months.

Day Two, early evening.

I decided to stay around the Edmontosaurus carcass for a while in case I got hungry again. I figured I may as well make that spot my home for a while. I spent some time exploring the surrounding jungle, trying to get my bearings and figure out if I'd need to move on. I drank from a small stream, flowing down a nearby rock, to wash down the last few chunks of rotten meat clinging to my teeth. There was also a dried lava flow which stretched far into the distance. I kept away from it. It looked like there was still lava boiling just beneath the crust and I didn't want to accidentally barbeque myself.

When I got bored of exploring I went back to the carcass. To my horror it was swarming with frenzied little feathered creatures, all of them tearing at the last strips of the Edmontosaurus' flesh. I bellowed at them and charged, furious that they were scavenging *my* meal. They glanced over at me with cunning slit-pupil eyes and darted away into the jungle, screeching and chirping at each other. I tried to catch them but they were way too fast and agile. They jumped over fallen logs, while I lumbered along smashing the smaller trees out of my way.

I soon gave up the chase and slouched off back to the Edmontosaurus. It was pretty much a skeleton now. The nimble little dinosaurs had picked it clean. There were only a few strips of flesh remaining and my mouth was too big and clumsy to get them. I don't know what the scavenging dinosaurs were, but I'd guess some form of *Dromaeosaurinae.* Basically, they were little raptor-like creatures – the sort of thing that would happily scavenge a meal and hunt smaller or wounded dinosaurs but probably shy away from anything that could put up a fight.

I went to sleep in a sulk. My stomach was growling again and I wasn't too likely to find another dead Edmontosaurus soon, especially now that I knew my new home was infested with bloody thieves.

Day Three, morning.

I'd slept for longer than I had done the night before, but again I woke up with a burning hunger. I knew that this time it wouldn't be so easy to find a meal. I'd have to hunt.

Now I didn't really know how to distinguish different dinosaurs by smell yet. I could recognise the various little creatures that always disappeared into the undergrowth when I approached. I also knew the animal stink of Triceratops and dead Edmontosaurus. I didn't want to try and hunt Triceratops in case I ended up trampled, impaled and very much dead and even my powerful nose couldn't detect anything I might be able to scavenge, so instead I followed a scent I hadn't come across before.

I'd already learned to rely more on my sense of smell than on vision. I could see what was going on around me and even pick out details, but I wasn't sharp sighted enough to spot anything hiding in the undergrowth. My nose on the other hand was fantastic and I followed the new trail like a bloodhound. Eventually it brought me to a wide open plain. There was nothing but gentle slopes and tall grass spreading for miles into the distance, only ending at a mountain range far on the horizon. I'd have stopped to appreciate the beauty of the sight…if I was human. As it was, all I really cared about was filling my belly and I could see just what I needed wandering about the plain.

All manner of herbivorous dinosaurs milled around in their herds. Some of them I decided immediately to steer clear of, Triceratops and the smaller Torosaurus could cause me a lot of trouble. Imagine if a rhino beefed itself up at the gym, then stuck even more spikes to its head…that's a Torosaurus. Now take that same rhino and make it even *bigger* and you have a Triceratops. I was smart enough not to pick a fight with just one heavily muscled, angry rhino-monster with too many horns. There was no chance I'd try and take on a herd of them. Worse still were the Anklyosaurus. They had no horns, but more than made up for it in thick, armoured scales and a bony mace on their tails that was large and deadly enough to make a medieval knight green with jealousy.

Basically anything armed with giant horns or a heavy club on its tail was out of the question. The Pachycephalosaurus were more appealing. They were smallish dinosaurs that loved to charge each other with their bony heads. I figured I could catch one before it managed to break my kneecaps with a well placed head butt. Still, there was an even better option open to me…a herd of Edmontosaurus. Nice, juicy and largely defenceless Edmontosaurus. Perfect.

Day Three, a while later.

Despite the growling and cramping in my stomach I made sure to take my time and watch the Edmontosaurus herd from the edge of the trees. I've seen plenty of wildlife documentaries where a hungry lion attacks a wildebeest too early and gets trampled. The trick is to watch the herd and target the slowest, weakest member. You separate them from the rest and bring them down.

I watched and waited for what felt like hours, but was probably only about ten minutes, until I spotted my target. It was an old Edmontosaurus with a nasty leg wound. It looked as though it had strayed too close to a Triceratops herd and been chased off by them, taking a horn in the leg along the way. This particular dinosaur limped behind its herd, just far enough away for me to separate from the rest.

When I was human I was a real animal lover. I even went vegetarian for a while, but just couldn't live without bacon. I still liked pigs and I wished bacon just grew on trees, but it tasted so damn *good.* I was in the late Cretaceous now though and I couldn't afford to be sentimental. My brain obeyed my stomach first. Any guilt or pity for the wounded Edmontosaurus would have to come later.

I waited for the perfect moment. Once I had a clear path to my target without having to get to close to any of the more dangerous dinosaurs I charged. I bellowed as I thundered out of the tree line.

The herds scattered in fear at the sound, exactly what I needed. The Triceratops and Ankylosaurus gave me a wide berth and the other Edmontosaurus ran directly away from me, leaving the wounded member of the herd behind.

I closed the gap in moments and collided with the bleating dinosaur with explosive force. Jaws powerful enough to crush bone closed around the Edmontosaurus' neck and silenced it in an instant. My prey collapsed to the ground and I roared my victory to the sky before tearing and biting deep into the dinosaur's belly.

As good as the rotting carcass had tasted to my Tyrannosaurus' palate, this was a hundred times better. Fresh, warm and bloody. Yes it might sound mean, it might even sound disgusting. If I was human I'd probably think that way, but I'm not human. I am a Tyrannosaurus Rex, King of the dinosaurs.

And I love it.

The Betrothed

N. M. BROWNE

TOMORROW IS MY WEDDING DAY. The festivities have already begun – for everyone but the bride. My father brought twenty barrels of ale as a betrothal gift so pleased was he to be rid of me. My guard snores at his post. I step over him, tuck my braided hair under my cap and sneak out into the dark. Kai, our hostler, promised he'd hide my sword and belt knife in the stables.

The cool, salt wind whips a stray strand of hair across my face. I shiver. It is cooler here than at home and my disguise does not include a cloak. I should have thought about that. I am tempted to borrow the guard's woollen cape, but he's likely to wake if I manhandle him. My lady mother says it is better to let sleeping dogs and dozing warriors lie; for once I believe she is right.

My father's ale has done its job and there is no one to stop me entering the cobbled courtyard. The gusting breeze brings the sound of singing – male voices belting out old marching songs. I can't help but grin at the words. My mother would stop my ears with wax to keep me from such vulgarity. She would love to keep me wrapped in wool and fine linen, as if we still lived in the safe world of her childhood, before the legions left.

The flames flicker wildly in the braziers that light the night. What is wrong with these men that they have not a set a watch? The moon is full though the night is cloudy. Tonight would be a

fine night for an attack and my betrothed has many enemies.

I keep away from the light, stick close to the stone walls of the main house and creep towards the horses and my weapons. Feast or not, I won't venture among men without them.

The singing stops and a harpist plays – old music from the wild places, tribal melodies that have found their place again. I open the stable door. Inside a lantern burns brightly. I am dazzled for a second and then rough arms grab me and the keen edge of a steel knife nicks my throat.

"Speak." It is not Kai's voice. I forgot that my betrothed has grooms of his own. The blade is colder than my chilled face and I swallow hard. I mustn't squeak my reply like a frightened girl. I raise my hands to show that I bear no weapon.

"I'm Gwyn of the Lady Morgana's company," I lie and am pleased that my voice hardly trembles at all. Whoever holds me withdraws the knife, but his arms still grip me tightly. He stands behind me so I have only an impression of a strong man a little taller than myself. I can see now that I have stumbled on a tryst. A girl about my age sprawls in the hay, her rich robe disordered. Her dark hair falls in loose curls to her waist. She laughs as she takes in my sack-like tunic and too short trews.

"It's only a slave-boy, Lance. There's no reason to fret. He'll not tell on his betters, will you lad?" She winks at me, brazen as you like. We've not yet been formally introduced, but if this is not my future sister-in-law then I am indeed a slave-boy. I hope she does not remember my face as clearly as I remember hers. My captor loosens his grip on my arm and steps into the light. He is startlingly handsome, tall and well built and, by his clothes, someone of importance. His dark, deep set eyes are dangerous. A man to watch.

"If you speak of this to anyone," he says, pleasantly, pointing his longsword in my direction, "I will geld you with a blunt knife."

I nod, grateful that I am in the shadows still. I lower my eyes as my servants do and wait to be dismissed. I watch him take the woman's hand.

"It's time. Go. Everyone says the Lady Morgana is a right old bitch. Watch out she doesn't find hay in your hair and the stench of the stable about you." He pulls the woman to her feet and kisses her hard on the mouth. She wraps her arms around his neck, entangling her fingers in his hair. I can feel myself blushing. How dare he speak of my mother with such disrespect? She has her faults, nevertheless she has kept me from men like this. I should be pleased, but I am not. I am to be married tomorrow and have never been kissed like that.

My almost sister-in-law leaves, smiling, a cat who has caught a mouse. The man turns to me.

"You can fight, Morgana's slave?"

I nod mutely. I have practised a bit with my dead brother's sword – nothing more.

"Take these." He hands me my own sword belt and I fasten it awkwardly around my waist. If he was surprised to find it hidden in the stable he keeps it to himself.

"Follow me," he says and I do. He is that kind of man.
He strides out towards the hall where the men are feasting.
Oh, by my Lord's precious blood! My father is there with all my uncles and cousins, our house guard and our servants. They are all blind drunk.

The Hall is packed; full of colour and noise – bright, woven hangings, painted shields and a multi-coloured mosaic floor. Burnished gold, gleaming silver and polished steel glint in the light of many torches. I have never seen so many men all together. The hall stinks of ale, roasted meat and male sweat – a heady mix. I try to sink into the shadows. I must not seem overwhelmed.

I don't notice him at first, my betrothed. I have never met the man, which is why I am out of my bed, dressed as a slave-boy, so that I can see what my mother's manoeuvring has brought me: so I can know the worst.

He is not drinking with my father, surely the duty of a future son-in-law at a feast. He is in the middle of things, the calm centre, the hub of the room. He wears a heavy gold torque of the kind the wild tribesman wear out in bandit country. It is much too big for his slender neck. He turns to speak to my companion and I see that he is a slight man, barely more than a boy, with straggly blonde hair in need of a wash and a smattering of spots on pale skin. He is short too – a good head smaller than me. He isn't handsome or well-built but something about him draws all eyes. I let out the breath I didn't know I was holding. I would not choose him, but at least he isn't loathsome. Unlike my father and his men he is sober as a black monk and all *his* retinue are as sharp as the blades they carry. I fear treachery.

"Lance, are we ready?"

My companion nods. "We should send your Lady's family safely to their beds," he says.

For one terrible moment I fear he is speaking of their graves. It would not be the first time a tribe has been slaughtered at the hands of their hosts. I tighten my grip on my sword but I am not foolish enough to think I could do much against these men – warriors all of them – even my skinny husband-to-be.

He speaks again: "Gar, Marcus, Hen, take enough servants to see our guests to their rooms. Be hasty. We've not got long." His voice is not loud but is swiftly obeyed.

My father staggers out of the hall leaning heavily on a young man. The rest of my relatives lurch after him. I am alone in this stranger's Hall, more frightened than I have ever been.

"I still think we should have kept them sober..."

I do not see who speaks.

"I wanted them out of it. It is my own men I want beside me tonight, not strangers."

"The worse the odds the greater the victory?" Lance says but my betrothed does not answer for at that moment an armed man stumbles into the Hall. He almost trips over his feet in his eagerness. All turn his way as he cries out: "They are coming!"

Lance orders me to follow him. He grabs a shield from its place against the back wall, dons the helmet he has left beside it and leaves the Hall at a run. Around me other men do the same and I am swept out into the cold like a gull on the sea, carried forward by the force of the tide. Whoever is coming will be met by spears and sharp blades.

"Sing!" My betrothed says and at once the men begin another raucous rendition of some soldier's song. They slur their words and laugh.

And only now do I see that a trap has been set: my much heralded wedding has been a lure for some foe cowardly enough to attack a feasting tribe. I am angry and afraid in equal measure. He doesn't want me any more than I want him; our marriage is a ruse.

I don't join in with the singing: it needs no girlish descant. Instead, I follow Lance's broad back as he leads us to man the wooden stockade that surrounds the villa. My father said it was a well positioned place and now I am glad of it. The stronghold is high on a hilltop with the sea to the west. Not an easy place to attack.

I think I can hear movement below, the chink of metal, the scuffling of climbing men. I can't be sure: the sound of singing drowns everything out. It swamps the sound of our swords hissing as they are unsheathed. Men ready their spears, strap on much-mended breast plates, secure dented helmets and keep on singing: in harmony.

Lance points at a wicker basket full of stones leaning against the wooden parapet. He signals for me to sheath my blade and hurl the stones down on the unsuspecting heads of this unseen enemy. I nod, hoping he can't see my fear. My hands are clammy with sweat and a trickle of perspiration runs down my face. If I survive this my mother will kill me. I'm not sure I can survive. I haven't thrown anything but tantrums since I was a little girl.

I don't see the signal that silences the song. When it stops there is no doubt: I *can* hear men climbing the steep scarp slope toward us. They are close. Then the moon emerges from behind a cloud and it is bright enough to see the silvery glimmer of metal.

"Now!" Lance slings the first stone hard and accurately. I hear the thwack of its landing and a man cries out. I can barely lift the boulder I must throw. My hands are too soft, too small, but now is not the time to act the princess. I grunt with the effort, yet I lift the stone and heave it into the darkness. I don't hear it land and I don't think I hit anyone.

"Quicker!" I do what I can. My fingers start to bleed, but I dare not stop. These climbing men are coming for me and mine and all my menfolk are unfit to fight.

It isn't easy to see. The moon is capricious, playing hide and seek behind the clouds. Lance is no longer beside me. I bend to lift the last of the stones and when I straighten up I am looking straight into the eyes of a warrior. I freeze as he raises an axe. I don't scream. I don't do anything.

He is going to breach the wooden wall. He is going to pull it down. I am going to die.

Christ's's holy wounds! I will not stand here stunned like a lamb before the slaughterer's knife. I still have the higher ground.

I heave the heavy stone and hammer it down on my enemy's head. Once, twice, then it slips from hands which are slick with my own blood. The man staggers backwards, stunned, but he does not fall and now there are other men there in the darkness surging towards me. I cry out. Nothing sensible, nothing useful, but it brings men to my side. Men who know what they are doing. A spear whistles past my ear and a man falls right in front of me. I hear his last gurgling breath though it is too dark for me to see him land. Tall figures surround me, push me back from the stockade. I want to run and know I can't: I am here and my father is not. There is not just honour at stake but life – all our lives. I unsheathe my sword and squeeze my way back to the wooden wall.

I have no idea what I am doing. The wall is falling now. I see a man pulling it down and I hack at his bare hands. My blade is none too sharp yet I don't give up. I duck a blow from an axe and stab at the white flash of a hand until its owner retreats, screaming. It is dark again. Something hisses overhead. We have archers! A man falls to my right. I hear the heavy thud as he drops like a felled stag. There are men all round me and I don't know which are my enemies and which my friends, if I have any, because it is already too late; the wall is breached and a gap like a broken tooth has opened up right in front of me.

"God's balls, lad, get out of the way." A man in a mail shirt shoves me roughly to one side. Wrong footed, I stagger and almost fall and the mail-shirted man takes the sword blow meant for me. The clang of sword against sword tells me that he has parried it. They are locked in combat, grappling with each other, grunting, panting. I want to help, yet in the darkness I can't tell who is who. The man who saved me delivers a killing blow. I do not see how and then there are more of our enemy pouring through the breached wall.

My sword is out and I follow him, my saviour, staying well clear of his sword arm but slipping beside him to help if I can. In the brightness of the moonlight I see the spear arc towards him and time slows. I try to warn him but there is too much noise – guttural cries and screams. I grab his arm to pull him clear, slip and slide on churned land that has quickly become mud and the two of us tumble together to the ground. The spear lands where he had been standing scant moments ago. He hauls himself back to his feet but not before I have seen his face and he has seen mine. That moon again, its bright light unveiled at just the wrong moment. After that the tide turns. I feel it even in my ignorance. We beat them back. Some run, or try to: all are swiftly caught.

When dawn breaks pale and grey, I can see the battered bodies of the fallen, streaked with mud and other things: few of them are ours. As men stack the corpses, I slip away back to my room. It is the morning of my wedding day and I have duties of my own.

Julia, my maid, widens her eyes when she sees the state of me and gets to work. I ache all over and my fingers are raw. Julia asks no questions. This place still has a working bath house from the olden days and we make good use of it. Julia oils and scrapes and cleans my body and my hair. She anoints me with oils and dresses me in all my costly finery. There is a cut on my face that is hard to hide so she arranges my braids to cover it. If she knows of last night's battle she keeps her own counsel. My guts turn to water when I think about what is to come.

My father comes to walk me to the Hall. His eyes are bloodshot and his skin, grey. He still stinks of ale,

"Your betrothed is a sound man, a bit quiet but sound. We fought off the Sais last night – it was hard – and he handled himself well."

I nod because there is no point in contradicting my father. He pats my hand, which is as much affection as he has ever shown me.

"He'll keep you safe and that is no small thing."

I think my betrothed is over fond of war and a ruthless gambler with it. My father has no idea how close we came to losing everything.

Lance is magnificent in his scarlet tunic and wolf skin cloak. I feel his eyes on me as I walk a little stiffly towards my groom. Neither he nor the other men show much sign of their night's work.

Then, suddenly I am through the throng, alone at the dais where he waits. He has washed his hair which improves him greatly. I was wrong about his height for we stand eye to eye. He is still wearing the mail he wore in battle, over a tunic of fine wool. Someone has sand-scoured the mail shirt well: it gleams as if it were newly made.

We stand side by side as the priest blesses us and joins our hands. Then he turns to me to say his vows. His look of shock when he sees my face makes me want to laugh. Last night he saved me and I saved him back – there are worse starts to marriage. He clasps my hand now, all formality gone. After all we have lain together – in the mud. He smiles at me broadly, his face alight, and he *is* handsome.

"I Artur, son of Uther, Count of the Saxon Shore, take you Gwynefa, daughter of Caradoc for my wedded wife."

I think this is going to be interesting.

Robin and the King

MARIE DENTAN

ROBIN LOOKED AT HIS PALM and sighed heavily. How could he have been so stupid as to believe that fortune-teller all those months ago? He had abandoned his work at the tavern, his family, the little he owned, and all for what? For nothing.

"*I see you with King Henry V,*" the fortune-teller had said holding his palm in her wrinkled hand "*I see you with the King, and a great procession coming back to England. I see everlasting glory.*" Then she had smiled a toothless smile and limped out of the tavern.

When he had heard that, Robin could not believe his luck. It was his turn now to become famous. For years he had had to hear his comrades brag about their victorious campaigns with the King. He was sick of hearing the name of Agincourt where Henry V had won against the French. He wanted to be a part of the great conquest as well. Although his tousled hair, his freckles and his slender figure did not mark him out as a hero, he was sure he was destined for a greater future than just remaining an under-cook in a London tavern. When he had told his comrades he was leaving everything to follow the King on his quest to France, they had laughed.

"You're too little and frail."

"You're not even fifteen."

"You can't stand the sight of blood. You won't last a day."

Yet he had gone, promising himself to prove them wrong.

Robin dropped his hands and sighed again. The fortune-teller must have been mistaken, there would be no glory for him. He was in France at the castle of Vincennes, with King Henry V, but the King was dead. A few days ago, the King had passed away from the illness caught at the siege of Meaux. He had fought his last battle against dysentery and had lost. Robin felt sad and cheated. Sad, because he loved his King, and cheated because the King's death put an end to his dreams of fame. The only glorious moments he could account for were a few evenings in the King's tent at Meaux. He had brought him food, and the King, who was a good man, had taken time to talk to him. Robin cherished those moments. However, this could hardly be counted as *'everlasting glory'*. What a fool he had been to believe that old woman.

"Enough with the day-dreaming. Follow me," shouted a voice.

Robin sighed one last time and followed his master. His master was a big-bellied bald man, the type who liked to cook and not talk. Robin tended to forget this last detail as he was more of the merry temperament and enjoyed a good chit-chat.

"Master, what is to become of the King's body? I have not seen any coffin being built?"

"He will be in no need of a coffin, boy."

Just as his master was answering him, a black cauldron on poles carried by four men passed them. It was big enough to cook a whole boar in it.

"What is that for?"

"It is for our King."

Robin stopped. Why would the King need a cauldron? He was dead. There would never be a meal served in the Castle again. Robin was about to ask another question, but he realised he had better keep quiet if he did not want to anger his master this early in the morning.

They arrived at the blacksmith's workshop which stood right next to the stables.

The two started talking together. Robin looked around at the knives on the workshop table. He was an under-cook, true, but the sort of knives that interested him were the ones that slayed people on the battle fields, and he was sure he could have done greater deeds than just bring food to the King.

"When is it going to start?" asked the blacksmith.

"When the bell chimes," replied the cook.

The master then turned to Robin. "Take this knife back to the kitchen, boy, I have some business to attend to."

Robin meant to go straight to the kitchen, but for some reason he stopped at the stables. He liked horses and most of all Henry V's horse. It was a white pure breed that normally held its neck high, but today it was mourning too. Robin went to it and softly caressed its mane. He started to whisper soft sorrowful words into the horse's ears. The horse listened quietly, rubbing its muzzle now and then on Robin's shirt. It was comforting for Robin to have someone to share his misfortunes with. Someone who seemed to listen and understand.

The bell chimed.

Robin jumped. He was supposed to have brought the knife straight back to the kitchen. He ran as fast as he could, hoping his master would not be there yet.

As he opened the door he was met by an angry hiss.

"Where were you? We could not start without the knife."

Robin looked at his feet. He did not say anything and gave the knife to his master. Then he looked around and realised something was unusual. Instead of the rattle and bustle that accompanied the preparation of a meal, the atmosphere was strangely quiet. Each cook stood in position, almost in contemplation. The only noise was the seething water coming out of the black cauldron. Robin was not sure he was supposed to be there, but he decided he had nothing better to do. And something amazing was about to happen by the look of everybody's face.

Outside the bell chimed.

All the cooks looked at the master.

"With the help of God, let's commence."

The master held the knife up high and hit the carcass. The blade made through the flesh in one sharp cut. Then the master passed the piece of flesh to a cook.

Then Robin gasped.

It was not a steak.

It was an arm.

Robin looked around in panic. What was happening? Were they so short of food that they had to resort to eating dead soldiers? He knew the last siege had been tough. He never realised it had been that desperate.

Then he heard a priest say words that made his head swirl.

"Benedictum Henry V, regnum in eternam."

Robin, desperate and horrified reached for his master.

"Boy. This is our beloved King that lies on the table."

Robin repressed a heave.

"We must retrieve the royal bones and bring them back, intact, to England. The only way to do this is to boil the flesh, so it will come away from the bones easily. If we left the body as it is, it would rot on the way home and be eaten by maggots."

Robin thought about being boiled or eaten by worms. He turned pale and ran out of the kitchen.

He was not a coward, but this was too much for him. In his head rang the mocking comments he had heard at the tavern. '*He will not last a day. He can't stand the sight of blood. What would he do on a battle-field?*' He had gone to France to prove them wrong, but

they were right. Tears blurred his vision.

Inside the priest was now singing a hymn. The music soothed Robin a little. For one second he thought this was just a horrible nightmare and he would wake up soon. But a heavy clang of the knife shook him. Robin fell on the pavement and put his fingers in his ears. *No, oh no, oh no!* He was not dreaming. Yet this could not be happening, not to his beloved King. The man who had treated him with so much courtesy was being butchered like he was some vile animal.

A horrible smell started to pervade the court. Robin could not imagine what was cooking inside and he did not want to think of knives or stirring ladles. However, it was all he could do to block images of the black cauldron and its deadly soup from creeping into his mind. He had to run away from the horror going on in the kitchen. He did not want to remember his King lying on a chopping table. To him, Henry V was forever the Warrior King. In front of Robin stood erect the Tower where Henry V had lived his last weeks. Without thinking anymore, Robin ran up to it.

Robin climbed up the stairs without breathing. When he arrived on the first floor he finally took a deep breath hoping the strange smell had not followed him. To his relief, it had not. He entered a room which must have been the council room as there were still some parchments lying on a huge wooden table. Here it was quiet and peaceful at last. Here no vision of ghostly flesh assailed him. The walls were richly carved with figures of angels and Robin walked slowly to one of the stools that surrounded the brown table.

His great King had sat in that chair. A King who had led an outnumbered army against the French at Agincourt, and had won against all odds. A King who was going to put an end to a war that had been going on for almost a hundred years between France and England. Robin closed his eyes and sighed. Besides all those great achievements, his Sovereign had had a good heart. Who else but Henry V could have had such great military success, and yet take time to be kind to an under-cook. Truly Henry V had been the best of Kings. Quietly tears ran on Robin's cheeks.

Outside, the bell chimed, and with this sound, Robin jumped as a vision of the seething black cauldron flashed in front of his eyes. He shuddered.

Then he heard his master calling for him. Robin was not supposed to be here, he knew it. He was getting into more trouble than he already was. He took one last look at the room and slowly walked down the stairs.

In the courtyard, Robin met his master and the horrible smell. Robin waited for the bashing of the ears he rightly deserved. Instead his master spoke softly.

"Robin, my boy, are you all right?"

It was the first time his master had ever asked him that question.

"We are paying respect to our King. You understand that?"

Robin tried to compose himself, but his tears betrayed him.

"You must pull yourself together boy."

Robin wiped his face with his sleeves. He was trying, he really was.

"Do you know what is going to happen to the bones afterwards? They will be put in a Royal Shroud and brought back to England in a procession. Knights and soldiers and a representative of each trade will accompany their King in his last journey. You, Robin, have been chosen to represent the cooks."

Robin looked at his master. Him, why him? He was just an under-cook, a nobody.

The master held Robin's shoulders gently.

"The King talked about you, you know. He remembered you

from the times you brought him food at the siege of Meaux."

Robin remained silent. The King had known who he was.

"He was a good King. It is a great honour to travel with him."

"I'm sorry Master, I'm not worthy of our King."

"No boy, you are, but you must believe in yourself."

"You don't think I am a coward?"

"Listen to your heart boy, not to others. Then you'll know who you are. Now I must finish the ceremony and strip the bones clean."

Robin did not flinch.

"Go fetch the Royal Shroud that Master John has mended."

The cook gave a good pat on Robin's back, ruffled his hair, and went back inside.

The bell chimed gently. Robin did not move for a few minutes. He thought about his comrades' mocking comments, and he thought about his master's words, and he thought about his beloved King. Softly, a breeze caressed his dirty cheek. Finally Robin took a deep breath, wiped his hands on his leggings and went.

When he arrived at the Tapestry's house, Master John greeted him with a big smile and a cry.

"For all the white angels in Heaven you look pale. No. You are not pale, you have a greenish grey sort of complexion."

Master John saw life in colours, and he was a good man.

"Come boy, come here, take this." He poured Robin a little glass of liquor. "It'll help you get through this day."

Robin took the glass and drank it. Fire burned his throat, he coughed and his face turned a lively colour of red.

"That's more like it," said Master John cheerfully. "Now let me fetch what you came for."

"How do you know what I need?"

"Oh, you are quite the talk of the moment, Robin. So young.

So young. What a wonderful honour my boy. It'll make your folks back home really proud. There it is."

Master John gave Robin a red velvet blanket embroidered with gold flowers. It was even heavier than the knife.

"Thank you Master."

"God be with you my boy. Fare you well."

Robin did not go back to the kitchen straight away. He had one place to go first.

When he arrived at the stables the pure breed looked up. Robin came up to it and showed it the Shroud. He was certain the horse understood. It ruffled its muzzle in the fabric and neighed a gentle neigh. Robin patted its mane again but this time he whispered soft comforting words in the horse's ears.

When he got back to the kitchen, the ceremony had ended, some incense was pervading thc kitchen and only the white bones remained on the table. Robin looked at them, but did not shudder. He gave the Shroud to his master, who laid it out respectfully. Then one after the other, each cook took a bone and placed it in the Shroud. Robin went last. Only the skull was left to lie on the soft fabric. He breathed once. He breathed twice. He took the skull in his hands and gently laid it down. The master folded the fabric and it was over.

Outside the Bell chimed one last time.

As Robin was washing his hands in the fountain, he suddenly looked at them. As the water was washing his palms clean, the whisper of a smile then a full grin illuminated his face. The fortune-teller had been right all along. He was coming back to England in a great procession, covered in glory. What a wonderful tale he would recount to his comrades at the tavern. How amazed and in awe everyone would be. Of course he might omit the part where he had run out of the kitchen, but after all, was it not the privilege of heroes to accommodate the truth a little?

The Hunting

LUCINDA NETTLETON

I WAS DREAMING AGAIN.

Dreaming of what I imagined she looked like. My father said I looked like her; untamed twists of jet hair and eyes as green as forest moss.

I saw her standing on the edge of a jagged cliff with only the wild sea to catch her fall.

She looked at me.

I looked at her.

She had fear on her face but love in her eyes. Her long locks blew in the wind like black ribbons escaping towards the moon.

One word crept from her parted lips…

"Kiandra."

It rolled from her mouth and floated into the air like a birdsong.

But then, before I could reply, she spread her arms and fell backwards; her silver robes tumbled around her like the wings of a flightless bird.

I raced towards the cliff's edge and looked down into the blue abyss but she had gone. The sea had claimed her.

I jerked awake, my forehead covered in crystals of sweat. The hut was dark and still except for a wisp of smoke that snaked across the room from a freshly burnt out candle.

Grenis was asleep in front of the door, an unmoving mound of fur. My father was asleep on the wooden stool by the cooking pot, his musket over his lap and an empty bottle by his foot; he often guarded the night from devils that moved in the darkness.

England had fallen on dark times. It was the year of our Lord 1646 and the land was ravaged by Civil War. While battles raged between the Roundheads and the Cavaliers, evil spawned in the crevices of the divided nation. In the absence of the Shepherd, the wolves feasted on the flock. No one was safe.

I covered my father with a grey, woollen blanket. He woke, his lips trembling as if it was not his daughter that stood before him but a ghost haunting the night. He moved his rough hand to my soft cheek; his eyes searched my face for answers.

"My love, is it really you?" his eyes filled with tears, "Oh how I have suffered without you but I have waited for your return."

"Papa?"

My voice startled him.

"Anna?"

His hands felt at my face, aiding his eyes that had been tricked by the darkness.

"Yes, Papa."

He shook his head, blinking away the image that misted his senses.

I knew who he saw before him.

"Why did she leave us, Papa?"

"Who?"

"My mother."

"She wasn't from these isles, Anna, you must understand that she had to leave us. Her heart was in shackles while she was away from her home."

The woman by the cliff flashed into my mind…and that word, what did it mean?

"Papa, what does Kiandra mean?"

He froze.

"Who has spoken that to you, my child?"

Suddenly, an orange glow started to fill the room, creeping through the windows, dissolving the darkness. The blaze illuminated my father's face.

It was growing larger, coming nearer.

Then, something cracked against the door, shattering the deadly silence, making the entire house quake.

My father grabbed his musket. Grenis ran to his side, growling from the pit of his stomach.

"We know she is in there!" slithered a voice through the crack of the doorway.

My father's silent hands ushered me to hide.

I scurried under the bed with the chamber pot ensuring my white nightdress was covered by the shadow of darkness. I prayed for the Lord God to protect us from the unholy hell that waited...

The Lord is my Shepherd; I shall not want. He maketh me to lie down in green pastures...

My father walked to the door.

He restoreth my soul: He leadeth me in the paths of righteousness...

His hand paused before the iron latch. He took a deep breath.

Though I walk through the valley of the shadow of death, I will fear no evil.

He flung open the door.

His eyes were met by those of a crowd of men, women and children; batons of fire in their hands which glinted across the pitchforks and scythes in others.

"Where is she?" called a voice.

"Who do you seek?" asked my father.

"The witch!" cried one woman.

The word booted me in the stomach; winding me, leaving me silently gulping for air.

Waves of fear engulfed me, burning at my flesh, making me retch.

A man at the front of the mob, with hooked nose and black eyes, stepped forward. I near screamed at the sight; it was him, the devil himself, the Witch Finder General.

I had heard stories about him that would make even the bravest blood curdle.

He leant forward and inhaled deeply at the air within our home.

"God help us all!" he shot backwards and crossed himself. "The air reeks of witch! We will not allow witchcraft! We will have no devil worshippers on our doorsteps!"

"Friends, you are mistaken." My father bravely called into the night, "There is none here but my dog and I."

"Lies," hissed a voice from the mob.

"He hides her!" cried another.

"The witch has been seen from your window; hair black as tar and eyes as red as Satan himself," yelled the Witch Hunter.

"I warn you to hold your tongue, Puritan," spat my father.

The Witch Finder General continued, "She will eat the babes of this village while they sleep in their cots!" He called to the crowd, then turned back to my father, "We must check her for the devil's mark!"

"Devil's Mark? Hokum!" shouted my father, "People, do not be tricked by this man. He would accuse the Lord God himself of Witchcraft if it paid a pretty penny."

"Blasphemy!" shouted the Witch Finder, "I tour the lands as a messenger of God; no witch shall sleep in the bosom of East Anglia while I draw breath."

The mob was a sea of demons. Their faces aglow in the

flames, with wild, unblinking eyes. My father searched the crowd.

"Master Scrivins, if your father was not fighting the King's Army, he would not allow you to follow this crook to my door…and you, Millicent," he pointed at a woman, "he could do the same to any of your daughters."

"Silence," shouted the Witch Hunter, "hand her over or we will burn your house to the ground sending you, the witch and your hell hound back to the fiery pits from whence you came."

He stepped forward. My father pressed his musket against the sagging, grey skin of the Witch Hunter's cheek.

My heart raced, my eyes were wide with fear for my father's life and my own.

"Your actions betray you, heathen," hissed the Witch Finder General.

He spat on my father's boot then turned to the crowd and shouted.

"This man hides the witch within his home and threatens me, a man of God, to protect her sinful life!"

The crowd gasped.

"He too is in league with the devil and must pay for his treachery! I condemn this man and the witch he conceals to be burnt alive!"

My father stood in the doorway; an unmovable force, with his musket ready to fire at any who moved against us. Grenis by his side, teeth bared and hackles raised.

The Witch Finder turned to face my father. His stooped back and sharp chin, half aglow and half shadowed, made him look more demonic than human.

"May God have mercy on your soul!" His eyes glinted as he grinned, revealing his brown teeth.

Then he slammed the door shut.

I shot out from under the bed and ran to my father's arms, trembling in his embrace, even Grenis circled us whimpering. We heard the mob edging around the house, lighting the bales of hay and grasses. The crackling of the flames grew louder as it devoured our home.

My father grabbed my hand and we ran for the back door. He pulled at the iron latch but the door wouldn't open.

"Anna, the key!"

I ran to my bed and pulled the blackened key out from under my pillow. I had started locking the doors to protect us from the very demons that had found our threshold tonight.

I ran back across the room when suddenly the burning reeds of the thatched roof caved in before me.

"Papa!" I screamed as I darted left and right, looking for a way past.

"Anna, you must jump through it!"

"I can't!" I cried.

"You must!" shouted my father.

I edged back to the front door, gripped the key firmly in my hand then charged at the hellfire before me.

I leapt through the flames and into my father's arms. He held me close as he fumbled the key into the lock. We pushed through the door, Grenis close on our heels, then waded through the mud of the pig sty at the back of the house. The pigs squealed in protest.

"They have escaped!" someone shouted.

"After them!" cried the Witch Hunter.

We jumped the fence of the sty and ran into the black forest.

My father ran ahead, pulling me through brambles as the trees watched down on us like soldiers of the night. Grenis ran at our sides, chasing the moonlight, darting between the tall oaks.

We kept running, heading for the coast at the far side of the forest. The horde chased us in the darkness.

I could smell the sea air.

"Don't let her get away!" one howled.

"She must pay!" screeched another.

We ran through the trees, branches clawing at our faces and tearing at our arms, but we kept running.

Suddenly, we burst out of the forest, bloodstained and breathless, the sea before us like an endless sheet of blue silk glistening in the starlight. It looked so calm.

"Come, Papa," I grabbed my father's hand and tried pulling him towards the cliff, looking for a jagged path in the rock face but the weight of my father anchored me to the spot.

He was staring at the sea and whispering to the horizon.

"Papa, we have got to go!"

I pulled at his arm with all my might but my feet just dug trenches in the mud.

The glow was getting nearer. It was nearly upon us.

"Papa!" I shoved him hard.

He spun to face me, his eyes filled with unspoken words. He grabbed my hands and pulled me close.

"Listen, we don't have much time." His eyes searched every inch of my face."Anna, you need to head to the shore. Someone will meet you there. I will distract..."

"No, Papa, You must come too!" Tears streamed down my cheeks.

He kissed my forehead.

"Anna, listen," he sobbed, "you will be safe. Trust me."

"But Papa..." I cried, my heart breaking with every word he spoke.

Grenis whimpered at my feet and pressed his furry head against my legs.

"I love you, my beautiful Anna."

"I love you, Papa."

All of a sudden, something flew out from the darkness and wrapped around me, knocking me to the ground.

"We've caught the witch!" cheered a voice.

My father scrambled at the net that pinned me to the earth but he was dragged away by the shadows.

I screamed after him.

They had sneaked up on us under the cover of darkness, leaving their flames in the forest to distract our gaze.

Grenis stood in front of me of me, growling and snapping his jaws at any who approached.

"Let me go!" I cried, "I am not a witch!"

"Silence!" shouted the Witch Finder General, "Hold your tongue, witch, unless you want to lose it!"

I could hear footsteps coming towards me, squelching in the mud.

Grenis growled louder but the shadows still moved in so he bravely charged into the night.

A yelp echoed through the night air.

"Gren!" I cried.

Then silence.

"Please," I whimpered but the words didn't make a sound.

The trees moaned as they were bent back and forth by the wind. Lightning streaked the sky in blasts of fury. I could hear the waves crashing on the rocks and felt the salt spray dampen the air. Then, carried on the wind, a voice shrieked into the night.

"Kiiiii- Annnn- Draaaaa," it howled through the heavens.

"Ki-An-Dra," it called.

"The devil has come to help the witch!" cried the mob, trembling.

"God help us all!" one screamed.

"Do not be fooled, good people, it is nought but witch trickery," shouted the Witch Hunter, stepping forward from the darkness, coming closer with each flash of lightning until his face was inches from mine, only the rope net between us. His eyes were black and his breath reeked of decay.

"Listen to me, witch," his words pushed through the net and into my ears, "tonight, I will end your sinful life!"

"But I am not a witch," I wept and searched his stone eyes for a shred of mercy.

"That is what they all plead," he spat.

"I am just a girl."

He turned to the people and shouted over the wailing wind.

"People, I have looked into her eyes; they are as red as hot coals and her tongue is forked like the very serpent that invaded the Garden of Eden. I say we hang her from this very tree."

As he spoke, I saw a noose being bound onto the twisted oak that overlooked the sea.

Men snatched me from the ground and carried me towards my death. I struggled against their grip.

"Anna!" my father's voice called but I couldn't see him.

"Papa!" I cried back hoping my voice would carry over the storm.

They stood me on a tar barrel and ripped the net from me.

I shivered in the cold, my nightdress blowing in the wind.

I could see them all through the noose that hung before me. They were uttering prayers to save my soul from the devil. I wept and searched their faces for compassion.

Someone please help me.

The barrel shook underneath my trembling feet.

I saw my father rushing towards me, fighting his way forward.

"Anna, Kiandra is your name," shouted my father. "It means…"

He fell out of sight.

"Papa!" I cried and lurched forward, the barrel wobbled.

My father's voice rose above the shouting.

"It means…Babe of the Water!" he cried, "Magic of the sea!"

The woman from my dream, my mother, falling off the very cliff that stood in front of me now flashed through my mind.

The crowd momentarily looked at my father. A narrow path ripped through them. I jumped from the barrel and forced my way through the people.

"After her!" cried the Witch Hunter.

But he was too late.

I leapt from the cliff, my body outstretched like a swan maiden, my nightdress fluttering in the wind as I cascaded towards the sea.

The sea was wild beneath me, the waves reached up like black claws. I swallowed my fear and held my breath just as I plummeted through the icy depths, into the belly of the beast.

"If she floats she is a witch," cried the mob.

But I kept swimming down into the depths.

A black figure came soaring towards me. I tried to swim from its path but it snatched me in its arms. My mouth opened in shock and the air escaped my lungs.

I tried to break free from its grip. I needed to get to the surface for air. I thrashed against its soft body until my lungs ached and I fell limp in its arms. I looked at it as I felt my life escape me.

It was a seal, a black seal and its eyes…

The eyes of the woman from my dream looked back at me. They were enchanting.

I closed my eyelids as the last bubble of air escaped from the pit of my being.

My heart was slowing, the panic had gone. I wanted to sleep on the sea bed.

The sea was silent. I felt calm.

"Kiandra," it soothed.

My eyes flicked open.

"Mother?"

The seal smiled and nuzzled my face.

"Kiandra, my daughter, I have been waiting for you."

I looked down at my hands but all I could see were flippers. I swam in a circle trying to see my entire body.

"I am a seal!" I cried.

"You are a Selkie," corrected my mother, "a seal by sea but a woman by land."

I wanted to burst out of the sea and dip and dive along the surface until I reached the horizon. I am safe, I am free.

But then I stopped, the parade in my heart died.

"What about Father?" I asked.

"Do not worry, child, he has nothing to fear now you are safe. See for yourself." She smiled.

Together, we swam to the surface to watch the mob from behind a seaweed encrusted rock. On land the storm had ceased and the crowd waited for me to pop to the surface; dead or alive.

After a while a little boy stepped forward.

"She must have sunk and died," he said.

"She wasn't a witch after all," sniffed a lady, hugging her children close.

They stood in silence for a moment.

"He said she was a witch," said the boy.

"Serpent tongue," snarled the woman.

The Witch Hunter was escaping into the forest when the crowd turned and spotted him.

"After him!" they cried and chased him into the woods.

My father and Grenis sat together on the cliff edge, quietly watching the sun rise over the sapphire sea, until we would meet again.

Thomas Goodman and The Great Fire of London

GUY VERNON

FROM WHERE I WAS STANDING it was difficult to see towards the east of the city, but the orange glow against the smoke darkened sky and the smell of burning tar and wood borne on the wind, told me which direction to go.

Before leaving, Mistress Agnes, my mother's maid, had hugged me tight, "Run fast Thomas, follow the directions I've given you and keep yourself safe." I smiled and stuck my chest out, yet even as I ran down Honey Lane I wanted to turn back, to leave with the rest of them, but if I did Mother wouldn't get the medicine she needed so badly. If my father were here, if he were alive, he would know what to do, he would not be scared.

I had barely made it two streets away before I realised I was being followed by one small person who should have known better. I turned a corner and hid in a doorway, pushing myself in as far as I could as I heard them get closer.

One step, two steps, three steps, "Aaargh," I jumped out, onto the back of my pursuer, "Got you."

There was a muffled cry as he fell to the ground. I turned him over, pretending to strike him.

"Thomas, please, don't hit me," he cried.

"William, I'm jesting but what in God's name are you doing?" It was Mistress Agnes's boy, some years younger than myself.

"My mother would never let me go and I wanted to see the fire with you."

"I'm not going to see the fire. I've to get medicine for my mother and I don't have time for this. You must go back."

"Please, I won't be a burden and I know where the doctor's house is so I could get you there quicker."

He had a point. Mistress Agnes had the handwriting of an insect and her directions were all but illegible.

"Very well, but we must hurry." Although I too was curious to see just how bad the fire had become.

People ran in the opposite direction as we made our way into the wide open boulevard of Cheapside. The smart shops and arcades were all closed and the streets themselves mostly deserted. Ash and smoke hung in the air.

"Thomas, look."

I looked to where William was pointing. Down towards the end of Cheapside was the Royal Exchange and yet I could barely believe my eyes. Its bell tower and wide archways were wreathed in flames, like some vast golden serpent wrapping itself around the building. Behind it a shimmering sea of fire surged, engulfing the surrounding buildings. Even from where we stood the heat warmed our skin.

"God have mercy on us," I whispered.

At that moment, as if the fire itself had overheard me, it leapt across two buildings on Cheapside, wrapping them in its fiery embrace. I backed away.

"We need to hurry," I said, "you're sure you know the way?"

"Yes." William grabbed hold of my arm, pulling me in the

opposite direction, towards St Paul's Cathedral. We ran with those people still trying to leave, past the smart arcades and stores, which stood implacable, awaiting their fate.

A few minutes later we were directly below St Paul's. I noticed booksellers and other merchants moving their possessions through the scaffold-covered entrance. I imagined that even if God would not keep them safe, then the stone walls should.

"Up here." William pulled me down a narrow side street. "Here, the doctor's shop is down this street." The buildings were closely packed together, their upper floors almost touching across the alleyway. We walked down the cobbled street before William stopped in front of the window of a small shop. Inside I saw an old man packing jars into a large bag. This must be the doctor. I opened the door and went inside.

The old man looked over to me, "Who the hell are you, boy, and what are you doing in my shop? There is a fire if you had not noticed."

"I – I'm sorry. I came looking for the doctor."

"I am he, my shop is closed and I am about to leave," he said dismissing me with a wave of his hand.

"But…" I said.

"Leave. Now." He shouted.

I was taken aback and stood for a moment, dumb and unsure what to say. My father wouldn't have stood for this, he would have surely challenged the doctor and no doubt used his sword if he had been insulted so. And yet that was also how he met his death and I was not my father. From outside I heard urgent cries followed by a rumble as if thunder were approaching. Unless I acted now, I would not get the remedy my mother needed and she would…

"Sir," I said, "I have a list of herbs that I need for my mother and you are the only man who can provide them."

"I have no interest in your request boy," he said as he finished his packing.

"Yes, I am just a boy," I replied, "but at least I am brave enough to venture into a burning city to save my mother, while you cannot find it in yourself to mix some herbs."

Now it was his turn to stand in silence. William fidgeted at my side. Had I gone too far?

"Hand me the list," he said. When at first I did not move he repeated, "The list, do you have it? We have little time."

I pulled the list out of my bag and handed it to him, trying to hide my shaking hand.

"Tis mine for sure," he gave an exasperated sigh, "very well, and quick." He took several of the jars from his bag and poured the various herbs and powders into a pouch. He then took two glass vials and filled them with brightly coloured liquids, "This should do it; the instructions remain the same." He took his bag and without even asking for payment, he left.

I placed the pouch and glass vials in my bag, using some brown paper to wrap them in safely.

The explosion happened without warning. There was a blinding flash which caused me to stagger backwards. William grabbed me at the last second as the front of the shop caved in bringing part of the ceiling down. A few moments later I looked over the edge of the counter. Where the window and door had been was now just a mass of broken wood and burning rubble, shards of glass reflecting the orange of the fire now burning nearby.

Smoke poured in through the gaps. We could not get out the way we came in. I noticed a door leading out of the room we were in and into the back of the building. I pointed and we crawled on our hands and knees to the back, the thick smoke making it difficult to breathe. As soon as we were through the door we ran along the length of the corridor. To our right was a dining room, six dark wooden chairs neatly arranged around a large table, place settings laid out for a meal that would now never happen. In front were some stairs.

We ran up several flights to the top of the house. There was just a small landing with two bedrooms on either side. I went into one of them heading straight for the window which I opened. The windows of the building opposite were barely an arm's length away. We could easily cross the gap. I grabbed a long pole lying on the floor and smashed it repeatedly through the window opposite, shattering the glass. I could only hope the building was deserted as this one was. I reached for a blanket and threw it over the edge of the broken window, before throwing my bag across, hoping that the contents would not break.

"I'll go first," I said, "and then you follow."

William nodded, not making a sound. I hauled myself up onto the ledge, pulling my feet up readying to jump across. I dared not look down. The height from the ground was dizzying. I took a deep breath, tensing my body.

Ready,

And,

Jump. I pushed myself off, landing with a small thud over the edge of the window. I pulled myself the rest of the way in and turned to help William across.

"William," I called, "your turn. Crouch on the ledge and then lean over. I'll pull you across."

He looked at me, shaking his head.

"William," I shouted at him, "do it now. I'll be ready."

He didn't move. His face was frozen and I saw his eyes close. *Please,* I thought, *move now.*

There was a loud creaking followed by a muffled crash. Smoke began to billow out of the bedroom window next to William's.

I heard him gasp as he backed away from the window.

"William!"

Thick smoke began pouring into his room engulfing him. It looked to me as if a shadow man had crept up behind William and wrapped his arms around him, smothering him.

"No," I screamed. William disappeared from view. My breathing came in fast bursts, my mind whirling in panic. I had to go. I couldn't stay. There was nothing I could do, nothing. My mother, she needed the herbs. I edged my way back, across the rug covered floor, my hand reaching behind me for the door I knew must be there. I stopped.

"Damn you William." I couldn't leave him. I left my bag on the floor. It'd be little use to me if I didn't make it. I pulled myself back across the gap, dropping into the bedroom. The smoke was thick and greasy. I coughed, momentarily winded. The building groaned as its burning timbers weakened.

"William?" I called, yet there was no reply. For a moment I lay there on the floor, the only sound that of spitting and hissing coming from the building. Then I heard it, a small whimper above the sound of the dying house.

"William?" I called again, yet this time I didn't wait for a reply and crawled across to where the sound had come from. I saw William's body curled up against an oak wardrobe. I grabbed hold of him.

"Move, now." I didn't have time to plead. I pulled him across to the wall, holding my breath before pushing him up against the open window, breathing in deep. "You either go across, or you drop." I hauled him up in one swift movement until he was half out of the window.

"No," William scrabbled into the air, kicking back, yet he had no choice but to reach towards the open window of the building opposite. As soon as William was safe, I followed. I reached across and held William tight for a moment.

"Sorry, are you alright?"

"I am scared of heights," he sobbed, "I thought I'd drop."

I smiled, "I wouldn't have let you. Now we've got to go." I grabbed my satchel and led the way down the stairs through the building, the sound of breaking glass from above telling me that the fire was behind us again. We ran down as fast as we could, through the kitchen and then finally into the narrow alleyway.

We stepped back into a world that had changed beyond all recognition.

In the near distance I could hear the cries of men and the crunching of timber structures being torn down. The air in the narrow streets was hotter, a harsh unnatural wind pushed against me. Angry black and orange ash clouds floated above in the sky.

"This way," and I pushed William towards the top of the lane. We ran onwards, the heat now funnelling through the narrow streets, winds buffeting us. Every so often a loud bang would ricochet across the buildings, adding to the confusion. We turned left into Fryers Street as fire belched out of the ground floor windows of a burning shop. Intense heat washed over us.

"Back," I shouted. The fire roared around us making it difficult to be heard. We ran back down the street, skirting around a burning, abandoned watercart. As fast as we ran, the fire outpaced us.

Down one road, a building collapses in flames.

Across another, timbers fall, our way is blocked.

Turn the corner, the street itself burning.

Hell's very army ran ahead, its foot soldiers torching buildings either side as we tried to outwit them.

We stood at a crossroads as I held William tight. Around us the city blazed, the glowing skeletons of homes spitting and cracking as the air above seemed to burn. There had to be a way out.

"Here," and I pulled William by his sleeve up a steep lane, one small passage yet to be devoured. The lane broadened out as we went further up it. Up ahead was a small church and I knew that I would be able to see more from the bell tower. Inside, the church was empty, rows of wooden pews facing an abandoned altar.

"Wait here," I said to William, "I need to see which way to go."

He nodded, sitting on one of the pews. I took the steps up to the bell tower two at a time, reaching the top in moments. What I saw made my breath catch in my throat.

"Oh God, no."

The flames were just a short distance away from the wide open square around the scaffold covering St Paul's. I saw people run as a sharp explosion ripped through the night sky, spewing fire and debris outwards.

I looked back from where we had come. In mere moments the fire had spread to within a short distance of where we were. I saw it now closer, leaping from tinderbox roof to tinderbox roof, buildings combusting in seconds. Yet there was a way out. I could see that behind the cathedral, there was a path. I went back down, into the cool of the church hall. William looked at me, his eyes watery.

"Can't we just stay here, the fire will not get this far, surely."

I knew otherwise, "I promise you we are almost there. We have to go now though." He looked so fragile, as if he would break at any moment.

We left the cool of the church hall and walked back into the heat. It felt as if the oven doors of some vast bakery had been left open. With great care we made our way downhill towards the huge bulk of St Paul's. There were more people now, merchants with loaded carts, desperate families with smoke blackened faces carrying what they could and heading west towards the city gates. As we ran a shout went up,

"The scaffolding, it is on fire." The flames had leapt across the wide plaza, igniting the wooden scaffold surrounding part of the Cathedral. We all looked back in awe, rendered mute at the sight.

There was a surge of movement away from the building as the spell was broken and we ran with the crowd our hands clasped together.

Eventually, the streets cleared and we made our way down the familiar quiet of Silver Street. Yet I realised this could not last.

In front of the house was a single waiting carriage. We rushed up to the front door, Agnes opening it before I had chance to do so. She collapsed onto her knees holding us both to her chest.

"I knew you would make it, oh bless you I knew you would," she sobbed.

"I have the medicine, where is mother?" I asked.

"They've gone ahead, we couldn't wait any longer," said Agnes, "I refused until you were back, but now we must go."

She grabbed a small bag of her own as I helped an exhausted William into the carriage. I took one last look towards the fire which, even now was rushing towards us, the heated wind ruffling my hair as it fed its fury on the streets and houses in between. Whatever I had been before I went into that hellish fire, I had come out changed. I had saved my mother and even though Father wasn't here to see it, no boy – no man – could have done any better.

"I did it," I thought, as I held my satchel close to my chest, my heart beating strong, "I beat you."

Riders' Business

JACKIE GODDARD

MATTI LAY ON HER STOMACH peering along the beach. From her hiding place between two rocks, she could make out shapes moving in the shadows of the secluded cove. The dipping sun lit up the coloured sands of Hunstanton cliffs, as if they had been freshly painted.

As daylight faded into evening, she watched the silhouetted figures unpacking two rowing boats. Her Maw would paddle her hard if she found her here – Matti didn't care. This was the closest she could get and even an ear bashing about lying on damp sand was worth it.

She heard someone running and held her breath as he passed close to her. A single word turned thrill to alarm as he hollered,

"Riders!"

Matti couldn't see them, but she could hear the sound of hooves on wet sand and knew instantly the danger that was coming towards her. There were shouts – cussing and crying – as the Dragoons pounded across the beach in the dimming light. The front riders held flaming torches to guide the way. Those who followed rode with swords already drawn and slashed towards every shadow. The horses splashed into the water as their riders urged them towards the fleeing boats. Matti lay frozen, unsure what to do except watch the scene unfold.

A man looked up as the alarm cry reached him. He dropped the crate he'd been lifting and frantically pushed the rowing boat away from the beach. The oarsmen responded instantly, pulling towards deeper water.

He didn't watch them go. Picking up a small keg, he turned and ran from the approaching horses. His boots slipped and squelched, as he tried to keep his footing, heading for the sand dunes, where it would be easier to hide. Matti lost sight of him in the shadows.

A flash of light and the crack of a pistol shot pierced the darkness, as someone scrambled near her hiding place. She jumped and cried out, giving herself away. Strong hands pulled her up and pushed her forwards.

"Move!"

The smuggler forced her up the beach and into the dunes, where he threw himself down and began scrabbling away across the sand on his knees and elbows, pushing the keg in front of him. Matti tried hard not to choke in the sandy dust he kicked back behind him.

"Come on! Afore they start perking around here."

She followed, trying not to stir up too much of her own sand, and shivered. The sea winds were bringing in a storm. A little further and they came across an upturned boat. The smuggler lifted it cautiously and crawled underneath. He flapped his arms to send Matti away and clutched the keg to his chest.

"Get you home girl! You have no business here."

He made himself as small as he could and pulled the boat over the top of him.

Matti looked at the row of cottages on the rise of the cliff. Two lanterns shone in the upstairs window of the end house where Maw had put them earlier. Keeping low to the ground, she crawled and rolled her way further into the dunes, until sea grasses turned the soft sand into a coarse carpet.

Half an hour later, she was wrapped in a rough blanket. Her damp clothes were drying beside the fire and her ears were ringing from the clip she'd received for being out late and coming back wet. She'd been given the job of stirring a pot of stew hanging over the hearth and the warmth soon put an end to her shivering.

The fire gave the only light and Matti loved the shapes it made as beams danced and flickered around the room. She smiled and wafted the flames to make the shadows skip some more. Her cousin Charlotte sat watching her with scorn.

"Whotcha gorping at?" Matti challenged.

"If you mean what am I looking at, then why don't you say so?" retorted Charlotte.

She spoke with hardly any trace of the Norfolk accent and Matti felt a surge of resentment. Normally she paid no attention to the way she sounded, but Charlotte's criticism made her drawl more than usual.

"Oh, listen t' you. I don't need you t' learn me how to talk, Miss High and Mighty lady!"

"I'd rather be a lady than crawl around in wet sand like a smuggler."

"What exactly do you mean by that?"

Charlotte raised her chin, "Everyone knows that respectable people don't go down to the beach at night."

"Guess your pa int respectable then. He's always down at the beach at night!"

Matti sneered at her and was rewarded by a flash of anger in her cousin's eyes.

Charlotte's father commanded a Company of King George

III's Dragoons and Matti could not be sure, but she guessed that it was his Riders who had been on the beach.

The shifting mud flats, rolling sand dunes and myriad creeks which fed the Wash made it easy for smugglers to land their goods and escape quickly. The work of the Dragoon Riders was often dangerous and her Uncle could be away for many days searching the shoreline and following trails. When this happened, Charlotte came to stay with her Aunt – and Matti.

"I don't think you'd understand at all," she said snootily. "What could you possibly know about Rider business?"

"I know more than you think," scoffed Matti and then realising what she had said, blushed and looked away.

At that moment, her mother came downstairs from the bedroom, carrying the two lanterns. It was clear that she had heard the girls' conversation and she gave Matti a sharp look as she hung the lanterns from hooks in the rafters. The shadows disappeared to the corners of the room in the new brightness and Matti noticed her worried expression.

Determined to change the subject, her mother began to issue orders.

"Serve out that stew, Matti. Charlotte, you fetch the bread. I don't want to hear you two bickering anymore."

"Yes Maw," they both said meekly.

Matti's mother was known as 'Maw' to everyone and she could control the toughest fishermen in the village with the same look she now gave the two girls.

Matti pulled a face and filled three bowls of stew. Handing one to her mother, she tried to have a private conversation.

"Why does she allus have to stop here?" she hissed dramatically. "She's right tetchy and she don't half run on at the mouth. What if you didn't move them in time?"

Matti flicked her head towards the lanterns.

Her mother waved her quiet.

"Sometimes you speak a load of squit, Matti. I just forgot to bring the lights down earlier, that's all."

Smiling at Charlotte, she added, "Pay no mind to her. She doesn't mean anything. You're always welcome here. You two really are going to have to find a way to get along."

The warning look she gave Matti was enough to shut her up and they ate in silence. But Matti knew that there was trouble ahead and she watched Maw pull her shawl tighter around her shoulders, throwing worried glances towards the rain-splattered window.

An hour or two later, they were startled by four quick taps at the door. Matti jumped to her feet and opened it, gasping at the heavy rain and cold air. One of local fishermen stood there and beside him was the smuggler from the beach. Both men were soaked.

"The Riders were out in force t'night. I have one for you."

"I can't," said Maw, coming up behind Matti. "We have someone here. I took down the sign, di'n't you see?"

"Please," he spoke in an urgent whisper. "There was trouble at the drop. It got nasty. One of the Riders got shot. Get him on the Peddar's Way tomorrow and I'll pick him up. But let him stay tonight."

Matti opened the door wider and let the smuggler in.

He stepped past her, glaring suspiciously round the room. Maw pointed to a curtain beneath the stairs.

"There's dry clothes in the chest. We'll get y' some wittles."

She flicked her head towards the fire where Charlotte was watching wide eyed in surprise. Matti shut the door and crossed the room to her.

"Ya gorping again," she snapped. "Don't just stand there,

get him some stew."

The smuggler came out from behind the curtain, pulling a dry shirt over his head and Matti noticed that he'd tucked a pistol into the top of his trousers. She shuddered.

"You'll have to kip in the chair," said Maw.

He didn't answer. Sitting down, he stared at the two girls. Matti took the bowl from Charlotte and gave it to him. The smuggler tucked in hungrily; all the while watching with eyes as dangerous as the lead shot he kept rolling between his fingers.

Matti shuddered a second time. She was used to strange and sullen 'visitors', as the smugglers were called. Most were just a bit rough and ready; some were quite fun; but the black narrow eyes of this man were crueller than any she had seen before. One of the Riders had been shot and Matti knew who by. Looking at Charlotte, she hoped she didn't make the same connection.

He'll be gone tomorrow, she tried to reassure herself. He'll be taken at dawn along the coastal path to join the old Peddar's Way. Then he'll be met and taken to Castle Rising, where he'll be picked up and hidden in one of the carts heading to the Market in Lynn. Then it should be easy to get a boat at the docks to wherever he wants to go.

The escape route for smugglers was simple and effective and Matti knew this because she would be the one to lead him to the start of the Peddar's Way in the morning. She had done it many times before. A man and a girl attracted less attention than a man on his own when the Dragoons were about. Normally she treated the whole thing as though it was an adventure, but not this time.

When Maw gave the smuggler another drink, Charlotte pulled Matti into a corner.

"Is he a smuggler?" she whispered with the same terrified look that she had worn since the man arrived.

"No, he's the King of England, stupid."

"Why's your Maw hiding him?"

"'Cos she is, that's all."

"But it's against the law."

"Hint it just! And I never knew!"

"But why? If the Riders catch you they will put you in gaol."

Matti's whispered laugh was full of scorn.

"Like we care. Ev'ry visitor we've help'd is one in the eye for the Riders."

"But my father is a Rider."

"Shut up whispering," said the smuggler and they sat in silence.

Charlotte's fear made Matti realise how different they were. Charlotte lived on the safe side of the village, where people pretended to be shocked by the smugglers and called them 'gentlemen' when they bought their black market goods. Matti's father had been taken by the Riders just after she was born. Maw had told her that he'd been hanged for helping an injured smuggler.

"Hanged for a caddy o' tea and a pinch o' baccy," she'd told Matti, "and for bothering with another human being in need."

Now they ran a safe house – a stopping place between the beach and the road to Lynn. Once or twice a month, when the small boats were busy bringing in their illegal goods, they would have 'visitors'. In return Maw received a small allowance from the local fishermen, who organised the smuggling.

Matti was well practised in what to do if a Rider came knocking on the door in the early hours of the morning.

"Wait you a minute," she would call, tousling her hair to make it appear as if she had just got up.

"I'm a-coming." Opening the door just a crack she would peer out and pretend to yawn. "What you after?" she'd ask.

"Is your mother there?"

"It's the middle of the night, Sir. She's asleep in her bed. She sleeps like dead, Sir. Even your pounding on our door hint waken her up. She'll not take kindly to be woken, Sir." Matti would whine a little more.

"If she's startled up, she might just quackle me."

She'd put her hands around her neck and mime being strangled.

Sometimes the Riders were very persistent.

"Do you have anyone else here?"

"Only my uncle, Sir," she would say with feigned innocence.

"Come t' visit, Sir. He hint bin well. No Sir, me Maw can't come, she's looking after him in case it might be catching."

Her job was to keep prattling at the Rider until he got fed up, but under no circumstances to let him in the house. It gave her mother chance to hide or disguise their guest. It was just a game. Now, as Matti looked at Charlotte's scared face, it didn't feel like a game anymore.

It was an uneasy sleep for everyone that night. Maw tried to send the girls upstairs to bed, but the smuggler wouldn't let her. He wanted to keep everyone where he could see them, he told Maw. They bedded down with blankets on the floor beside the fire instead and although Matti tried to stay awake, it was impossible and she drifted into sleep.

When Maw shook her awake and pushed a beaker of steaming liquid into her hand, she tasted the nectar of a rare cup of tea. Rubbing bleary eyes, she looked at where Charlotte still slept beside her.

"Time to go." Maw spoke to the smuggler, who was helping himself to a small linen sack from under the stairs. Matti opened her mouth to say something, but closed it again when he glared at her.

She gulped the remainder of tea not wanting to waste any of it and grabbed her shawl.

The storm had blown itself out and the bitter cold of the dawn blew the last sleepiness away as they set out along the cliff top. The smuggler held her hand tightly.

"Take me back to the boat," he ordered.

"That hint the way we need to go," replied Matti, but he insisted and they turned down towards the beach and crossed the dunes until they came to the upturned rowing boat.

The smuggler lifted it up effortlessly. Beneath the boat was the keg and he prised out a knot of wood from one end. Putting his fingers inside, he pulled until a panel came loose. Matti gasped in surprise. He took out two oil skin packets and pushed them inside the sack he'd taken.

"What are they?" she asked, as the smuggler repeated the process at the other end of the barrel. "Tea? Baccy? Spices?"

He didn't reply and when two more packets were stowed carefully in the sack, he grabbed her hand and they began to make their way along the beach.

"Hey!"

A shout stopped them and Matti saw her uncle riding with two Dragoons by his side. When they reached them, her uncle dismounted. The buttons on his red uniform glinted in the early morning sunlight. His eyes were as steely as the smuggler's.

"It's a bit early to be out and about," he said.

"We're, erm, cockling," said the smuggler.

"You don't have a spade." Her uncle smiled at such an obvious lie.

"It broke. That's why we're heading home."

"Ah, that makes sense. You won't mind if I look in your

bag then?"

The smuggler frowned.

"It's just a broken spade. We haven't got anything else. We'd best be on our way. My missus will have breakfast ready." The smuggler gave a hollow smile and took a couple of steps past the Riders, pulling Matti with him.

"Just one more thing," her uncle spoke with polite calmness and winked at her, as the smuggler turned back.

"Could I please have my niece back – if you don't mind?"

The horror on the smuggler's face, as he looked from Matti to her uncle and back again was priceless.

He pulled her like a shield in front of him and backed away from the Riders, still clutching the sack. At the same time, he drew the pistol and fumbled for the powder he'd need to fire it.

Matti knew he could not hold on to her and load the pistol at the same time. She wriggled to throw him off balance and he pushed her towards her uncle. The two mounted Riders drew their swords and circled behind him, to block his escape.

Matti ran at the smuggler and jumped on his back, wrapping both arms tightly round his neck. She hollered into his ear and kicked her legs for all she was worth. The smuggler dropped the pistol to wrestle himself free of Matti's arms. As she fell off his back, her uncle hit, and by the time she was back on her feet the Riders had secured him to one of the horses.

Her uncle picked up the sack and examined its contents. He gave her one of the packets with a smile and another wink. "You'd best keep that," he said to her. "I think you'll like it better than cockles. Tell your Maw that I'll be round later for Charlotte."

Matti stared at him surprise, then sniffed the packet and smiled. Tea. She tucked it into her belt and grinned.

Lucky Hits the Skin

MATT KILLEEN

WHEN I PULLED ON JOSEPH'S JACKET for the first time I realised no one had cleaned it; the blood had just dried right on there, all round the big hole. I liked it. Brown blood, brown patches, black dirt… the drummers of the 111th have red coats like the men and if you ignore the faded gold stitching I don't just look like a British soldier, I look like a real, proper Spanish veteran.

They call me Lucky. When I was born no one thought I'd live long as I was all stringy and yellow. Even Mom put me to one side expecting me to croak, too weak to cry properly but too stubborn to die. She shouldn't have been pregnant following the army anyway, let alone giving birth in camp. There were rules about what soldiers' wives on campaign could and couldn't do. So when the Regiment fought a battle and won, then found me still alive when they returned, they said the victory was because of me. The Padre told me the truth was that the French were outnumbered and still gave us a real bloody nose that day, but that's not how superstition works.

Then a few years back, I all but died of the fever. The army was retreating through the snow back into Portugal, with no time to stop. Our battalion was lagging behind the others, dragging me and the wounded like baggage, expecting the Frogs to pour down on us any second. But they didn't. Napoleon got a whipping at

Corun-ya and out of nowhere I got better. As far as the men were concerned our survival was all down to me. It didn't matter how many of the British had died, I was special, I was the charm. I was Lucky. It's never you that gets killed, it's always someone else. 'Not me, not today'.

That's what everyone is thinking as I march into battle with them for the first time. Today I become one of them. Today, I become the drummer boy.

I'm not 'only' a drummer boy. It's a man's job; there just aren't enough men. I'm a British soldier at war, kicking the Frogs out of Spain. Military work, military discipline, military pay and of course, military deductions for uniform, equipment, nasty food and wet blankets. In theory that's always applied, being born in the camp to a soldier's wife and trailing after the battalion my whole life – being 'On The Strength' they call it. But now King George gets to take my money out of my pocket personally. As for the danger, just ask Joseph. Except you can't.

The Padre always says, war is simple. You line up in a field. You do what you're told, immediately and without a word. They use cannons, you lie down. They send the horses, you form square. You fire your musket faster than they do and you win. I know this is what he's saying to the three new recruits as I approach them. I've heard it a thousand times. Mostly we win, mostly it's that simple.

He looks up and sees me.

"And what time do you call this? You're late for lessons."

"Lessons? With a battle today?"

"Most important lesson of all, young Francis. How to stay alive."

Only the Padre calls me Francis. He wasn't a real priest. Not anymore at any rate. No one knew for sure why an educated man of the church ended up among the 'scum of the earth' – the beggars and drunks and criminals that made up the British Army. Everyone had a theory. Most think some judge thought it better to hand him over to the army than hang a vicar. Not that this would make him unusual. No one was here by choice, not even the volunteers. Didn't make him unpopular either. He was a good sergeant, kept his men alive, didn't beat on anyone unless he really had to.

"You know your signals?" His voice is stern. I nod. "Form square?" I rattle out the signal rhythm on the drum. The nearby soldiers look up and grin. One of them calls out.

"You see cavalry Lucky? See a Frenchman who's going to put a big sword up your arse?"

The men laugh.

The Padre leans in so his face is close to the new recruits and speaks quietly.

"Ignore them. They're making jokes so the fear will go away. Infantry is scared of Horsemen, but you remember that signal, if the men form a square, you're safe. Never, ever run. You're just making it easy for them. They're looking to ride past you and backswing their sabre into your face and you'll never see it coming. But if you form square, if you remember that signal Francis, nothing, not Satan himself can hurt you. Understand?"

We nod. He turns to me. "Here, I have something for you." He holds up a piece of chain. "Got this off a Frenchie saddle. Give me the drum."

My drum is a heavy beast. More than two foot deep and a foot across, it's a navy blue tube, crisscrossed by string and with the regimental crest painted on the side. It too has been patched up with daubed canvas and one large hole surrounded by splintered wood awaits repair. I struggle to swing the straps from my shoulders and stumble slightly. The men chuckle again. The Padre lifts it

easily from my hands and fastens the chain across the bottom skin and then taps the head. It makes a crashing noise like a fight in a kitchen.

"Now all you have to do is hit the skin and they'll hear you in hell."

The Padre says that a good soldier doesn't need to know why he's fighting, but this is what I learn off the other drummers. There's a big, fat Frenchie army marching towards Baadahofftth to break our siege and we're going to stop them. That sounds nice and simple to me.

Turns out war isn't that simple. Turns out if there's enough light to see the whole battlefield and the mist has burned away, then the cannons start and wrap everything in thick grey smoke. It's all guesswork and gossip. The French are moving. The French have stopped. The French are riding in on elephants on stilts. Our flanks are protected, our flanks are in danger, the battle is miles away. The rags keeping our powder dry are staying on our muskets today or we're the last regiment between the French and London. No one knows anything and those who say they do are liars.

So we all march forward. Stop. We march back. Stop. We all swing to the right, a complicated and messy process that leaves us looking like a dog's back leg and has the sergeants screaming. All the while, I drum. I drum the march, I drum the halt. I drum the retreat. I drum the... swing?... an order that leaves the drummers staring at each other in open-mouthed uncertainty.

And then there's concern, anxiety, panic. Mounted officers charge across the hillside through the gloom calling and waving. The lines of soldiers close up, men ready their guns. The word is passed down the line. The French are here. I look down the double row of red coats and see the Padre, passing from man to man. A shout here, a hand on the shoulder there, checking the muskets with a smile or a harsh word. He looks up and sees me. He winks but as he does so, there's a grain of doubt and fear in his eyes. I look around and see, with a hunger-pang of fear deep inside, that everyone has this look, from the grizzled knife-scarred veterans to the rich and pampered officers.

The band starts up and I join in. Among the smashing, crashing, crumping and booming of the battlefield you can hear the bands and drums thumping their way through a dozen competing songs and marches. Each one is saying this: hear me play. I am not carrying the wounded or clearing the lines of dead. All is well.

There are shadows in the smoke and shouts down the line. From the darkness looms a blue multi-headed monster, with a thousand pounding feet and a hedgehog coat of spikes.

The French approach, their own strange marching tunes now audible. I look at our lines expecting us to fire, but still we don't. They are close now. Close enough to see the individual Frenchmen fiddling with their muskets, all pigtails and unkempt hair, uniforms as patched and tatty as ours. And still they come.

Fire.

Turns out war is sums. The French fire and reload. We fire and reload. One, two, one, two. After a short while we fire again before the French can. One two, two one, two, two. And on it goes.

War is definitely noise, from the first explosion, through the rattle-shout and cackle of reloading, to the rolling thunder of volley fire, screams and crying. I see and hear none of this. All I see is the nearest man's face disappear in a red cloud and the uniform that it sat on crumple slowly to the ground like a puppet with cut strings. Then I watch him lie on the ground, arms and legs all wrong, a big hole where his head should be. This is all I see. Over and over again. I shiver as it grows cold and dark.

Then the men are all advancing, fixing bayonets to their muskets.

"Are we winning?" I shout, but no one can hear me. I hitch the drum strap up and stagger after them, trying to get into sync with the others. The troops break into a trot and begin to shout.

A fat raindrop hits my drumhead. Then I feel another. A moment later the men in front of me are lost in a curtain of falling water. My coat is immediately soaked, the ground seems to dissolve to a river under my boots and the sounds of the band are instantly muted. The water collects inside the rim of the drum and every beat throws up a tiny fountain over my hands. The shadows of the charging line look like dancing drunkards by the fire, but grey, and dark, and black.

I stop my ragged march. I'm confused like I've just woken up. I don't know where to stand. I don't know what's happening. I don't know what to do. The drum strap is rubbing the wet coat into my skin and tearing at my shoulder. I try to rub water out of my eyebrows and poke myself instead. I'm surrounded by crying wounded that I don't know how to help, watching shapes dancing in the rain.

I drop a stick. It spins off the rim and I try to catch it, but I miss and lose my balance. The weight of the drum pulls me forward and my foot slides away. The stick splashes into the mud and vanishes. I sprawl in a puddle, my feet skidding along the wet ground. Something heavy smacks into my back and hail the size of musket balls fill the air, the sound of their landing drown out everything. I curl up around my drum and close my eyes. My life has been full of certainties, even when that certainty was hunger, or cold, or discomfort. I am no longer certain of anything.

The music stops. I look up. The figure of a horseman forms between the hail stones. For a moment I think it's the Colonel but the silhouette is wrong. The horse crashes past me, the wind of its movement pushing me back into the mud. The cavalry trooper standing in the stirrups is a blur of navy and gold, his red cuff swinging a sabre in a wide arc, swishing over my stovepipe hat. Saddle, haunch, tail and he is gone.

I climb to my feet using the drum and through the easing rain I see the 111th running towards me, frantic, directionless, terrified. Among them, dozens of Polish horsemen.

I stand up in the chaos and I'm suddenly calm. I take my one remaining stick and begin to hit 'Form Square'. I don't know if I'm being brave or I'm too scared to move. I just...stand there, beating the order over and over again as the enemy cavalry break into the gallop and crash past me on either side. Their blades are doing things all around me. People I've known all my life are being cut. I see a few brave souls turn and line up a shot, but the muskets don't fire, their powder too wet. I look away as the swords do their work. Form Square...Form square...

Directly in front of me a straggling trooper is urging his horse into a canter. Like me he is now well behind the first line and his targets are few. I try not to look at his face, but below the weird flat-topped crimson hat and above his moustache I see his eyes narrow. I look down...Form Square...Form Square...I look up. He is cantering right towards me, standing in his saddle, his eyes fixed on mine...I look away...Form Square...I'm breathing heavily and my arms are beginning to shake, the beat is becoming frantic and broken. The panic is rising in me like sick. In my head I hear the Padre speaking...*Don't run from cavalry, They're looking to ride past you and backswing their sabre into your face and you'll never see it coming...*I look up. He is twenty yards away and driving his horse into a gallop. He lifts his sword…

I turn and try to run, still banging out a frenetic Form Square as the drum bounces up and down against my knees. My eyes start to fill with tears and I try to wipe them with my sleeve. The damp, rough gold lacing cuts at my cheek.

I can hear the hoof beats behind me, the panting of the horse and the jingling bridle over the distant screams. The smell of wet horse and dung fills my nostrils. I wait for the sword to cut into my neck… *backswing into your face…* the thudding in the ground starts to mess up my run and I lose the beat on my drum. The heavy breathing is next to me, then in front of me. The bared teeth and muzzle of the horse appear in my eye line. *Backswing their sabre into your face.* Ears. Mane. Shoulders. Glint…

I heave the drum into the air. Before the shoulder straps pull it down, the sabre smacks into it. The drum is almost sliced in half but the blade catches and stops dead. I'm dragged forward by the motion of the horse and off my feet, nearly pulling the trooper out of his saddle. He curses and tries to shake the drum free, but it spins away from him as I turn upside down, hauled backwards through the mud, the beating hooves just inches from my head. He grabs at the horse's mane to keep balance but it screams and twists away. I bounce off a hillock and finally his wrist-strap snaps.

I hit the ground heavily, followed by the drum and its buried sabre. We tumble along the earth and come to rest, my face first in a puddle.

I hear the trooper swearing as he pulls up, the horse staggering and complaining ahead of me. I start to scramble to my feet, my boots sliding hopelessly through the filth. When I push my hand across my face to clear my vision, it comes back scarlet red. The horse is fifteen yards away and the trooper has dismounted. He is staring at me rubbing his wrist. The drum is still hanging by its straps, the sabre hilt and point sticking out of it on either side. The drumhead is loose but whole, my sticks long gone. I pat out a dull Form Square with my hands. He begins to stride towards me. I take one step backwards and then stop. I feel hot blood dribbling down my top lip, so I wipe it away with my cuff and pull myself up to my full height. He stops in front of me, a towering anger in crimson hat and riding trousers. I pat out the rhythm again, my hands shaking so much the order is unrecognisable.

With a growl he grabs the hilt of the sabre and kicks his boot against the drum. The sword tears out of the shell in a shower of splinters and I sprawl back into the mire.

He stands over me, haloed by the rain that seems to fall from directly behind him. The blade hangs in the air. I look into his eyes, grit my teeth and bang my hands on the remains of the drum. Form Square.

The man frowns and raises the sabre. Then stops. His face clears and his body sags. Wincing, he slides the blade into his scabbard and rubs his wrist.

"Dobry Boże. Ty to jesteś dzielny chłop..." he mumbles turning away and walking back to the waiting horse. I sit up. He is going. The trooper mounts and gives a brief and alien salute before trotting away.

I sit waiting for my hands to stop shaking. The rain stops. I climb to my feet and start walking. I'm not alone. The ground is littered with dead and wounded. I try not to stand on any bodies but the carpet of redcoats gets thicker, the red facings of my regiment more numerous. So no one formed square. No one heard me. I have to stop looking down for fear of seeing someone I know but my vision blurs as I start to cry again. This time I can't stop.

This is why I almost walk into them. A voice calls out.

"It's Lucky!" The call repeats across the formation and a cheer breaks out. In front of me is what's left of the 111th, in a rough and ready square, surrounded by dead horses and troopers. I'm too tired to march the last few yards and don't want them to see that I've been crying. The Padre steps through the line of bayonets and marches over to me. The cheer grows.

"They heard you Francis. When the panic was at its worst, they heard your signal. Well done boy."

Then he looks down at my drum, the massive gash of torn wood, broken strings and split paint. "What, in God's name, have you done with that? Have you any idea what they cost? You'll be a grown man before you finish paying that off."

Deductions. At last I'm a soldier. But I'm better than that, I'm a drummer boy.

The Silver Spoons of Ordsall Hall

KIM HUTSON

RICHARD DIDN'T KNOW WHY HE'D DONE IT. He'd only wanted to help his mam, that's all.

The courtroom snapped into focus as the judge spoke.

"So, Master Richard Stansfield, please could you tell us your account of the events that took place on the 11th June this year 1831."

They'd arrived at the old Hall that day at the crack of dawn. It was midsummer. The mist clung to the fields in the rising sun. The two lads were a dirty smudge on the clean country scene. Their footsteps made a self-conscious thump, thump on the bridge that spanned the moat to the front door. Richard's master, Tom, had banged on the door as always with the handle of the chimney brush and Jones, the manservant, had answered promptly as he always did. The house was quietly alive with servants who scurried back and forth with breakfast dishes. The smell of eggs and toast made Richard's stomach gripe; he had never eaten a breakfast like that – he was lucky to get those things for supper. Even then he'd have to share with the other climbing-boys in the workhouse. Some of the servants in the house were probably no older than Richard, but he was so small and dirty compared to them. He pulled self-consciously at his tattered sleeves in an attempt to cover his arms. Tattoos crisscrossed his limbs; scars stained black with ingrained soot and tar from the chimneys he had to scramble up day-in, day-out.

Jones led them to the kitchen past the staircase where there hung a huge portrait of a stern looking grey-haired man with thick black eyebrows. His jacket was red and he seemed to tower over the banister, glaring at and judging all who went past. Richard had not realised he had stopped to stare at it, so he jumped forward when Tom gave him a shove from behind, "Get a move on, lad." A small and nervous girl clattered past them with the last breakfast tray as they entered the kitchen.

"Please excuse the commotion," said Jones, "Master Markendale has been called out early to tend to some business. We shouldn't be in need of the kitchen any longer though so please proceed as usual."

With a slight nod, Jones backed out of the room and closed the door.

"Come on then lad, up the chimney with you." Tom whipped Richard around the back of the legs with the long handled brush and gestured towards the still smouldering fireplace. Legs stinging, Richard placed the sack for collecting the soot on the kitchen floor and with a set of brushes over his shoulder and a brief leg up from his master, scrambled up the chimney.

Metal handles formed a ladder in the bricks that lined the chimney and they were still unbearably hot, even through gloves and shoes. It was impossible not to burn his knees and elbows on the walls. He could hardly breathe and the only light to see by was the tiny glow of daylight from the opening at the top, so he mainly did worked by touch – feeling the hot ash on the bricks. He scraped and brushed the layer of thick black soot off the inside of the chimney, especially in the bends, otherwise it might cause an avalanche that would blacken the kitchen or even worse; the soot could catch fire inside the chimney and burn the place to the ground.

Beyond the sounds of his chiselling and his own heartbeat, Richard could hear the muffled sounds of Tom moving around below.

"'Eyar lad," Tom's voice hissed in echoes up the chimney, "Lad!"

Richard felt something prod his shin. He looked down. He could see the edge of Tom's head and his reaching arm holding a package.

"What is it?" said Richard.

"Never mind that lad, didn't you tell me last time that there were a loose brick up there?"

"Yes, a bit further up though."

"Well go stash this packet up there then and quick." Tom's face disappeared as Richard took hold of the package. He could feel it was something hard and metal – it felt like spoons. Not wanting to be thrashed later, Richard did his master's bidding and shimmied further up, showering black snow onto the hearth below. He hoped the package would fit. He hooked his fingers around the hot brick and with a scrape it fell, wedged between his forearm and chest, singeing through his shirt with a smell of frying bacon. Richard almost dropped both the spoons and the brick but managed to slip the package into the hole in the wall. His shaking fingers forced the brick back into its slot.

"Done it!" he shouted. Tom's face reappeared under him.

"Shhh, squirt, shut it!" He looked around furtively, "Hurry up anyway, I'm off to the lavvy but I expect you to be finished when I get back." His face disappeared and Richard heard the door opening and closing. He quickly scraped the last of the soot down and clambered out of the hearth; a skinny black mess in front of the fireplace. The room was empty.

Clearing up, he smelt a different sort of burning above the soot and wood smoke – was that pipe tobacco? The hairs prickled on his neck and a strange chill crept down his back and legs. A heavy hand slapped onto his shoulder and almost stopped his heart. He jumped and looked round. With a warm waft of that smell of tobacco and the cold of surprise in his stomach, Richard faced a man.

He was tall with silver hair and black eyebrows; his red jacket was old-fashioned and stood out starkly in the kitchen. It was the man from the painting, Richard thought – he must be the master of the house.

"Hello there, my boy," he said and paused for a second to look Richard up and down.

With heels clicking on the flagstones the man turned and paced the room. When he got to the back wall he turned around, looking Richard straight in the eye. "I know what you've done, boy." His voice was deep and gravelly and although he was well spoken, his accent was broad, "I know where you've stashed the spoons and I think you should own up, don't you?"

Richard swallowed, trembling; he nodded. He gripped the handle of the broom for reassurance. The man took a pipe from his top pocket and using a match from his other pocket lit it and pulled a few big puffs of sweet smoke.

"Well I daresay your master will give you a thrashing if you tell. I saw what happened. But you should know better."

"W-why Sir?" Richard had found his voice, "Sorry Sir."
He hung his head and waited for a slap.

A slap did not come. "You should know better, boy, because you should respect this house and its masters, and that includes our property." He took another puff of his pipe and blew a plume of smoke across Richard's face. His lungs were so used to smoke that he did not even cough.

"M-Mister Martindale?" Richard questioned.

"Markendale," replied the man, his eyebrows furrowing with thought, "I think you'll find it's Markendale, but my name is Richard."

"That's my name! I'm called Richard, too," he exclaimed, then looked down, embarrassed, still awaiting that slap.

"Well a finer name there never was, lad," the man said, warming. "Well, Richard, what's to be done with you? I cannot go up that chimney myself I think you should own up and retrieve them."

Richard expected the man to stay and reprimand him in front of Tom, to shame him and make him apologise – then they would lose their jobs here and Tom would thrash him raw when they got back to the workhouse.

Tom burst in through the hallway door.

"Come on lad, what you playing at, that floor's not goin' to sweep itself." Then came the slap that Richard had been waiting for. He looked around ashamed and embarrassed. But the old man had gone.

Tom opened the bag for him to sweep the remaining ashes into. "They've give' us a beer for all our hard work, get it down you, don't be ungrateful." Tom thrust a tankard into Richard's throbbing hand and elbowed him so he slopped a quarter of it onto the floor. "Ey, mind how you go," he said and downed his own drink in one. Richard followed, gulping to soothe his tarred throat and to hide the look of concern on his face. He was still in shock after his encounter with the man: the other Richard.

They were walking along Ordsall Lane on their way into Salford when Richard summoned up his courage and asked his master.

"Tom, why did you want me to hide those spoons?"

Tom stopped in the road and stared accusingly at Richard.

"Why'd you think, lad?" he replied, "We can sell those and give your mam some money." He looked away across the fields and started walking again,

"Me mam?" said Richard, "You'd really give her the money?"

"Well, yeah, the workhouse got their money's worth 'an't they lad, you're a good little worker – gotta pay her for that 'an't we." Richard looked down and kept walking. He hoped that was true, but what he really wanted was to see her.

"But what if we get caught, Tom?"

"Lad, don't ask things like that, we won't get caught, they was just some old spoons – won't miss 'em, rich folk as them."

"But the man, he saw us, he knows what we done."

Tom stopped and turned. He gripped Richard by the arm, "What man?"

"Th…the man in the red coat, w…with the eyebrows."

"Ha, the man in the painting? Don't be daft lad."

They were at the Pendletons', in their usual positions, when the policeman called. Richard, wedged up the chimney, heard muffled voices and suddenly Tom's face appeared beneath him for the third time that day.

"They say we have stolen some spoons, dost thou know anything of them?" He was using his best voice again, thought Richard. So many thoughts popped into his head. Richard shivered. Police. The old man at Ordsall Hall. Had he reported them? Would he ever see his mam again? He imagined her disappointed face.

"I do not," shouted Richard, trembling on his perch. The guilt and terror was pulsing through him now. He was shaking so hard he thought he might fall down and tumble out in a dirty mess onto the hearth. The guilt was overwhelming. His voice came involuntarily:

"There is a loose brick up the chimney." He could hear Tom swear in frustration.

Richard stood in the box, at the Salford mid-summer session, 4th July 1831. Cuts and burns still sore on his chest and legs…and pipe smoke lingering fresh on the air.

"So, Master Richard Stansfield, please could you tell us your account of the events that took place on the 11th June this year 1831," the Judge repeated.

"Um, y-yes Sir." Richard eyed the faces that surrounded him. There was Jones, the manservant, next to a very important looking man with a moustache. At the back sat his mam, wearing her best hat and the look of disappointment he so dreaded. Tears pricked his eyes, but he forced them back.

"Yes, I were up the chimney at Ordsall Hall when Tom thrust upon me a package to hide. I…I thought it was spoons but I went to hide it anyway, on account of that he is my master and would have given me a good hiding after if I didn't." There was a murmur in court and Richard saw his mam dab her eyes with a hanky.

"Was there anyone present at the time who can validate your claim?"

"Pardon, Sir?" said Richard.

"Did Mr. Thomas Grafton force you to hide stolen goods?"

"Yes, Sir."

"Did anyone see it happen?"

"There was a man, Mister Martin…something, he told me to come clean or he would report me himself."

The judge looked across at the well-to-do man with the moustache, standing next to Jones, the manservant.

"Mr Markendale, can you confirm this claim?"

"No, your honour, I have never seen this boy in my life."

Richard was aghast, that wasn't the man he had spoken to at all.

"Not *that* Mister Martindale," Richard interrupted. "I'm sorry, Sir, but that is not the man I spoke to." The judge smirked and looked around.

"Well who, pray tell, did you speak to?" The courtroom was silent, all waiting to hear his answer.

"I spoke to the other gentleman, Sir, the one with the silvery hair and the black eyebrows, in the red coat – the one in the portrait in the hallway. He said he was called Richard, like me."

The faces of the crowd grew confused, and a murmur rose around the court.

"Order!" shouted the judge. "Mr Markendale, please can you come up and tell us what the commotion is. The man pulled at his collar and straightened his moustache before walking to the stand.

"Ahem, well, um, the thing is you see, the thing is that the man in the portrait is my predecessor, your honour. He is indeed called Richard, Richard Alsop – he held the lease to the Hall before me. The thing is, without meaning to sound at all mad, the boy could not have spoken to him, your honour, because the good man died over fifteen years previous."

"That cannot be!" shouted Richard, "I saw him, smelt him with my own nostrils your honour! He was definitely there, he put his hand on my shoulder, gave me the fright of my life he did!"

"You are a fantasist, child," said the judge. "The man you describe is dead and on that premise I cannot believe what you say. The court hereby orders you to two months' hard labour as punishment for your crimes."

In the darkness of the cell, Richard lay awake on the cold floor. Tom was in the next cell snoring loudly. How could he sleep?

Richard could not stop his mind from racing. His mother's sad face seemed to float on the air every time he closed his eyes.

The sound of keys broke through the fug of thought, jangling crisply through the darkness. Tom carried on snoring.

A candle came into view and a warm glow moved towards the cell throwing shadows of the bars across the dirt floor. The warden's eyes shone in the light. He raised a finger to his lips and unlocked the gate as quietly as possible. The gate creaked. Tom stirred and then carried on snoring.

Richard lay, frozen. The dark figure beckoned with a frustrated hand. Richard got up stiffly, his joints clicking in the stillness. The man turned and started up the gangway leaving Richard to follow the candle's glow.

Once outside in the lobby he breathed a sigh of relief.

"Wait here," he said and disappeared around the corner to the office. Richard heard the metallic crunch of a bag of coins on the wood of the desk and a grunt of thanks from the warden who quickly reappeared.

"You are free to go," he said.

Richard's heard was pounding as he walked tentatively around the corner, unsure as to who might be waiting for him there. A figure stood at the counter, shrouded in a long brown hooded coat. At first he did not know who it was but as a black shining ringlet escaped from the hood and the eyes came into focus Richard's legs became lighter. He skipped towards his mother and hot happy tears escaped his eyes.

"Mam!" he shouted, "But, how?"

She caught him in a huge embrace, tears of her own wetting his hair; she cradled him like an infant and kissed his dirty face.

"Oh Richard, my boy," she said, "Richard, I'm so sorry."

"I missed you, Mam, how did you come and get me?" He

sniffed back a sob.

She took a deep breath and stroked his face, "It was the man, Richard, the one you told of in the courtroom. Richard, he came to see me at home and he told me where the money was – his money. He said you deserved an education and an home. So I goes to get it and, Richard…" she took a deep breath, "Oh my boy, there's loads. Enough money in there for us to buy a little room and for you to not 'ave to sweep those blasted chimneys."

Richard could hardly breathe he was so overwhelmed. Over his mother's shoulder, through the tears in his eyes, he thought he saw a blur of red in the doorway to the dark street. He blinked to clear them and there was nothing there. Just the rain on the pavement and the sweet tar smell of pipe tobacco lingering on the air.

The Passenger

KAT WILLIAMS

WHAT WAS THAT?

My eyes snap open. The cloud of sleep has completely dispersed. I cannot have been dozing for more than a few moments, yet I could be wrong. I do not know how I managed to fall asleep, after all this is the first train journey I have ever taken. Nightmares from the previous nights along with the gently swaying motion and Father's warm, soft shoulder must have helped my eyelids close.

Father places a hand on my knee. He smiles, a pipe hooked into the corner of his mouth. Little clouds of smoke rising up towards the ceiling like a miniature version of a steam engine puffing away. His tobacco pouch remains in his hand, faintly perfuming the air, the smell comforting me. He whispers into my ear, "It was just the Conductor's whistle that startled you. Two more stops, through the tunnel and then we will be there, safe and sound." He gives my knee a little squeeze.

I gulp and smile back, trying not to think about what will happen when the steam engine enters the big, gaping hole of darkness. It reminds me of the story of Jonah and the Big Fish. Once you're in there's no way back, unless it decides to let you go free. Goose pimples travel up my arms in waves. I can feel the prickle against my blouse. I push closer to Father, seeking the security and reassurance that only he can give. I hear the gentle ticking from the pocket watch that hangs from his vest pocket.

Since he told me about our trip, I have been so nervous. One moment I am full of excitement ready to burst, the next I am frightened. It's all George's fault. He says that when a steam engine enters a tunnel, it does not come out again. And that it takes you to hell!

I wish I hadn't told him that Father was taking me on a holiday. I've never been away from home before. But Father's already been and met everyone. He has promised me that I will feel at home where I'm going, that everyone I will meet is kind and that they will look after me while I stay there, wherever 'there' is. I don't think he is staying with me. He tells me that there will be other children, just like me and that most of all they will stop these dreams I keep having. They are not dreams. I am not asleep when they happen, so how can I be dreaming?

Although what George said frightened me, I was not going to disappoint Father. He has been eager to take me for so long now. He says it's the best place for me. But not only this. Father has also promised me that there will be no more ice baths. Good. They make me want to cry and scream and lash out all at once. I cannot understand why he forces me into them. Sometimes he pushes my head in first. He thinks that these baths will make my mind work 'normally'. There is nothing wrong with my mind and I know that Father does not enjoy doing this to me. I can see it in his eyes.

The train jolts and the sound that follows it is deafening.

Jumping inches above the cushioned seating, I nearly land on top of Father's knees. I knock his pipe with my elbow and hear the soft clink of pipe against teeth.

My heart thunders. My breath judders and I've even stopped breathing. My eyes dart towards the narrow, carriage window.

There is nothing different about the window. The cream

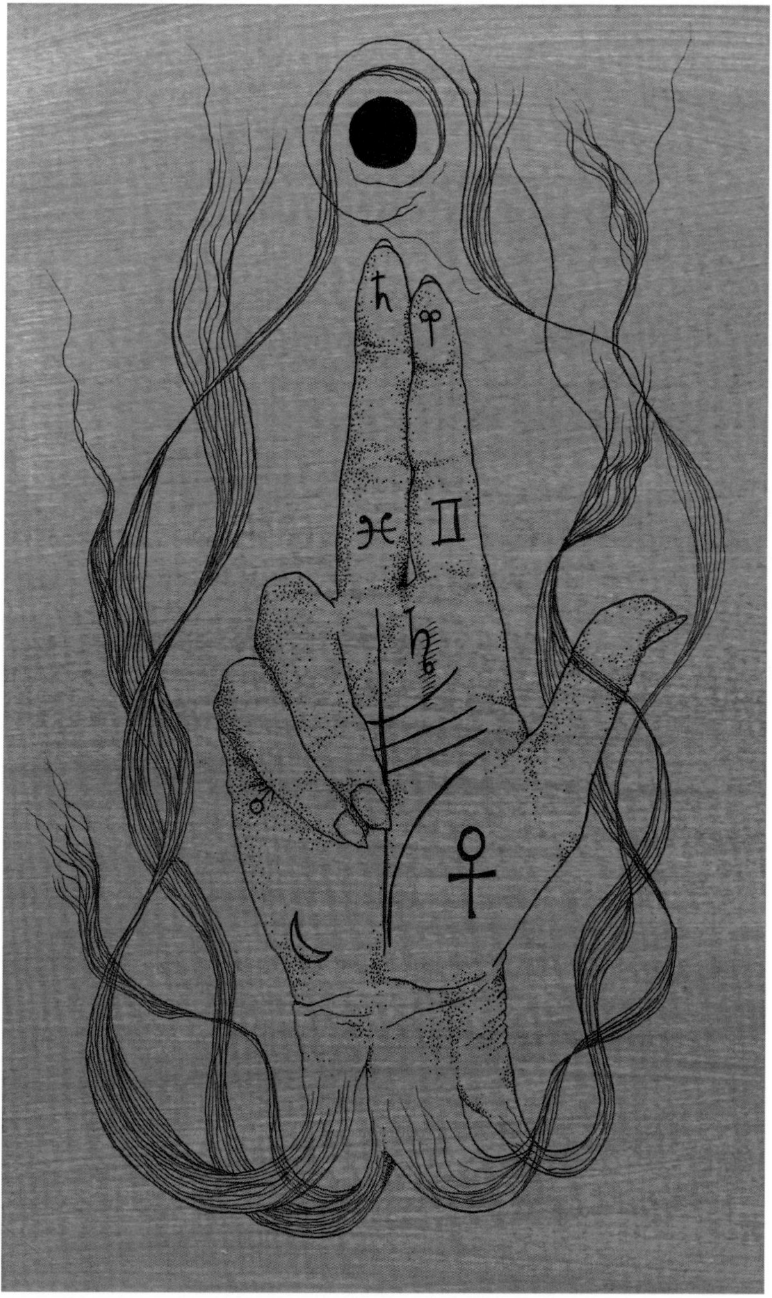

coloured curtains are still tied back and the greens of the countryside are still whipping past.

"Nell," my father calls gently, "it was just the thick brambles. Sometimes the hedges and trees can become a little overgrown. No need to be frightened. Nearly there now."

I exhale slowly.

Father softly half lifts and half pushes me back into the empty seat beside him. He stands up; his knees crack as they straighten. His body sways slightly as he gets used to the motion, even I can feel that the rhythm of the carriage is slowing.

The brakes screech and you can hear the steam leave the pipes. I can even picture what it looks like from all the times I have waited on the platform for Father to arrive. Being immersed in the steam, smelling the harsh burning coals and feeling the hustle and bustle; passengers struggling with their heavy luggage as they try to step down onto the platform and others trying to step up. Watching a train from the outside is so different from being an actual passenger.

Father stands by the partially open sliding door. "I will only be a few moments, Nell. Remember though – do not let anyone in this compartment. There are plenty of empty ones and because of the weather, some of the lower class passengers that we saw in open topped carriages... well, they will more than likely try to accompany us." The tone of his voice has changed. It is one that I imagine he would use with his students. He places his hat upon his head. And with that he is gone.

For a moment, I feel at a loss. I lean on the arm of the seat and stare at the door. My gaze moves to the floor as I follow the pattern on the carpet with the toe of my black shoe.

SNAP.

The cabin door slides open with a great force. Father was

quicker than I thought he would be. I lift my head to greet him, but the figure standing in the doorway is not him.

The figure is a woman. I do not know her, but she is achingly familiar.

The woman's skirts fall in folds, fabric upon fabric. Her shoes are hidden by the gathered pool of her skirts. Her corset is tightly pulled in, emphasising her narrow waist. Unlike her skirts, her corset is black, embellished with sequins and beads. The light reflects from them. A dark woollen shawl is worn like a hood and covers her shoulders. Its tassels hang down and are moving in the cold chill she brings with her.

Her gaze fixes onto mine. Her eyes are dark brown, framed by dark eyebrows. She reminds me of an owl, her expression severe and unmoving. She sees everything. She sees me and I see her.

One hand moves from her side, causing a soft jingling sound as it pulls the door across, sealing us both within the carriage. There is a tell tale click of a lock.

She smiles.

I am not frightened. She sees inside of me and isn't frightened of what she sees. To her it seems I do not have a disease of the soul. Something I have heard my Father murmur when he does not think I can hear.

Her hands remove the shawl from her head and her long hair is dark and shiny like a magpie's coat. The youthfulness of her hair is a stark contrast to her weathered face.

Father told me not to talk to fortune-tellers, let alone share a compartment with them. What am I to do? She is blocking the only exit; her stance is one of purpose. I sense that she will take no nonsense from me.

A whistle blows and a deep male voice shouts in the distance.

I feel the lurch of the train as it pulls forward. I can hear the accelerating clack of iron wheels on the metal work.

She steps forward, closing the gap between us. Not waiting to be offered a seat or to ask if there is room for her, she takes her place next to me. The comforting smell of my father's tobacco has been replaced by a sweet yet sickly smell of incense. It is not a strange smell to me. It is as though it is familiar but from a time long ago. I cannot grasp who it reminds me of.

She goes to take my hand. I want to pull away but I cannot.

I expect the chill of her skin to burn into mine yet I can feel the warmth radiate from her palms. My own hand begins to relax into hers.

"And what is this?" she purrs. Her accent is not one I can place. Her fingers stroke my skin and then extract something from my hand, as though performing a magic trick. I was unaware that I was clutching anything but between her long fingers is a stiff piece of card. My train ticket.

I can see the bold, heavy lettering;

GREAT LANCASHIRE RAILWAY
SINGLE
FIRST CLASS
MANCHESTER (OXFORD) to LEEDS
28th SEPTEMBER 1850

She places it on the space left in between us.

I notice that there are chalky black imprints where her finger tips have touched the parchment.

My hand remains clasped within hers. She has a firm hold on me. The other hand is reaching within the layers of her fabrics. From there she pulls a deck of cards. Colourful and elaborate designs appear upside down to me.

She does not shuffle these cards but instead places the deck next to my train ticket.

"Now let me show you something, my dear, Nell. Something that nobody is aware of yet, not even you. Something that is very real."

How does she know my name?

Her hand slices the pack into two even halves and the new tower is placed next to the old one, face down.

Her body turns to mirror me.

She grips my palm in both hands. Her olive skin is crinkled across her joints and each finger is decorated with gold jewellery, just like her wrists.

Her lips part as she begins to mumble.

Her eyes have closed but you can see the wavering movement behind them. The more I see her face the more it reminds me of…

I blink.

It happens so quickly. There is a dense, grey cloud. I cannot see clearly; it is as though I am looking through a pane of glass that has not been cleaned for years. The fortune-teller still holds my hand. Her mutterings have slowed down a pace but the language she speaks now varies, punctuated by the odd English word. At first I cannot make it out but then I hear the words 'bleak grey walls'. She repeats it, quietly at first, then strongly, finally ending with "Yes. I see grey walls...and locked doors...endless corridors and chains...and cages. Cages for animals they say. Isolated. This place has so much unhappiness. It is evil." She pauses as if hesitating, "Nell, the place you are being led to is evil. You're being led like a lamb to the slaughterhouse. Your father is wrong. There is nothing wrong with you."

My nose picks up the smell of burning, burning coal.

"The asylum is not for you," she whispers.

"Asylum," I whisper. The word leaves a bad taste in my mouth. I have heard about these places, but only a little. The stories I have heard were terrible.

The cloud begins to thicken. It is so dense that it leaves me spluttering. Ash is falling from the ceiling, fluttering to the ground like snow. I look down at where my feet would be on I look down at where my feet would be on the carpet, the cloud clears slightly and I see burning coals, their embers spluttering. Flames begin to grow, burning brighter. There's a fire, reaching out towards me, its fingers are stroking the flooring, the edges of the seats, the walls, the door frame. Long, thin gnarled fingers.

Panic erupts inside me.

The fortune-teller still has hold of my hand. She is rocking backwards and forwards, muttering faster and faster. I hear the odd word, "Disaster... robbers... tunnel... in the tunnel... fire... so much fire.... so much loss. We are heading into disaster."

Where is my father?

The image comes back into focus. I am in our carriage but I cannot see Father. A gold object shining through the smoke, catches my eye. Father's pocket watch! Lying on the floor is Father. His face is ashen and his eyes are closed. Small splutters weakly escape from his lips. His right arm is reaching towards the cabin door, a little flesh exposed. I, though, am nowhere to be seen. My place on the plush cushion is empty.

The scene in front of me changes again.

This time I am not on the train.

Instead I can see the train in the distance rushing across the countryside. The maroon red of the carriages is like blood seeping across the green fields. The sound is deafening as the wheels clatter along the iron tracks. I look further ahead down the line and see a tunnel that strikes a mountain through its heart.

There's a tug on my wrist. I am back in the compartment. My attention is back on the fortune-teller. Her head is leaning back, eyes still closed.

I realise that I am seeing the future. The train that I am on is not going to make it to its last stop. A fire will stop it in its tracks.

"Let me save you!" she screams at me. "I can save you."

The train is approaching the mountain. It's seconds away from the tunnel. This must be *the* tunnel. The tunnel where disaster strikes. The train is heading into the mouth of the mountain, taking all its passengers prisoners.

Whistling wind fills my ears with an orchestra of clattering wheels and steam pistons.

I want to scream.

I look from one scene to another. I see my crumpled, vulnerable father disappearing behind a curtain of thick smoke and then the crimson train racing into the tunnel which is then quickly replaced by the fortune-teller rocking backwards and forwards muttering repeatedly, "We cannot help him. Let me help you. We cannot save him."

I bring my hands to my ears, shutting out all the noise that surrounds me. No more cracking and popping of the fire or the distant screams and shouts of the other passengers in the distance. I even close my eyes, hoping to banish the chaos I am witnessing. Through the thin soles of my shoes, the vibrations of the train seep through.

The pressure that had been building up inside of me feels like it is draining away.

There is a pounding on the door.

"Nell! Unlock this door." It is Father's voice.

The fortune-teller's eyes are fixed, staring into mine. She is still. So still in fact, that for one moment I wonder if she has scared herself to death for I know that she has witnessed everything that I have just seen. There is the smallest movement of her head, as if she is nodding at me.

I tear my gaze away from the fortune-teller, whose face is no longer the olive colour it was when she entered. She now looks cold and grey.

The knocking on the door continues.

I expect to see smoke leaking under the doorway and into this small space. But there is no smoke. There is no glow from the hot embers and no licking flames. The floral smell of the fortune-teller has replaced the smell of burning.

Everything is as it was before.

I pull my hands away from her. There is no strength left in her grip. I go to stand but it is as though she has snapped out of some sort of trance and she is on her feet before I am.

I do not want her to go. Not yet. There is something about her which makes us connect.

She takes the cards that she had brought with her.

Two steps and she crosses the compartment. She unlocks the door and goes to grab the handle. I flinch, thinking that it will burn the skin off her hands but then I remember that there is no fire. It was just an illusion.

She slides open the door and is gone.

The sooty fingerprints remain on my ticket and in her haste she has left one card abandoned on the seat.

It's like she was never there. But she was. She was real. As real as me.

I go to turn the card over but my attention is distracted by my father talking. "We are near the tunnel, Nell. Are you ready?"

He smiles at me. A wicked smile. The smile of a devil. How can he take me to such a place?

The sight in front of me turns my insides cold.

Suddenly we are plunged into darkness. We have entered the tunnel.

I hold my breath.

From nowhere a hand grasps my wrist. Strong familiar hands, the rings dig into my flesh.

George was right. The tunnel will take you to hell.

Thicker Than Water

PAULA WARRINGTON

"IF I EVER CATCH YOU down by that Fleur-de-lis inn again, Charlie, so help me–."

Dad hung up his tar-black nightstick, with its golden 'Victoria Regina' and royal crest, and placed his top hat on the table. He didn't bother to tell me what he'd do: our dad is a man of few words. Our mam had a lot more to say on the subject as she threw my boots – thick with the evidence of open sewers – out into the front yard.

"There's a bad element down that part of town, Charlie. I really don't know how the women scrape along, when their menfolk are always drunk as boiled owls and ready for a dust up. The bother they've had at that inn!"

"But Mam," I argued, "the innkeeper started the trouble when he put up that sign. He says he don't like boarding-house types–."

Mam sighed. "Lord knows those poor folk have had it rough." She broke off to fuss around Dad, brushing imaginary dust from his uniform. Dad paid her no mind as he opened the evening paper.

"And I can't begin to imagine what it's like, being driven from your home by famine. But they're a bad influence, Charlie," Mam continued. "We don't want you picking up their slang and their wicked habits. Good morning, Mrs Jones!" she trilled through the open window to a neighbour who was passing down Thames Street.

Mrs Jones gave back the ghost of a smile. She waved a lace-edged handkerchief in front of her face as she got within sniffing distance of my boots. I think the neighbours can't decide whether a sergeant in the Leicester Borough Police is respectable enough for Thames Street. I'm certain they don't think *I* belong there. They probably wish I'd spend *more* time down Belgrave Gate, where the drains always seem to flow the wrong way and pigs in every yard add to the ooze underfoot. True, the place smells bad. Really bad. And when the ground is hard with frost and the pigs are killed, hot blood rushes down the gutters sending steam into the air. Luckily there's not much of a pig that don't get eaten, because any leftover bits end up in the street, too, and that don't improve the smell any. But the houses are higgledy-piggledy and the streets full of dark corners and jittys – and, once you get used to the smell, it's the perfect place for a lad of thirteen to muck about. So long as no one catches you and tells your dad, that is.

Being the son of a copper has its ups and downs. There's many folk won't raise a hand to me because I'm Frank Tarratt's son. And the kids who club together to buy penny dreadfuls – well, I think they're a little in awe that I'm on nodding terms with Tanky Smith. (Everyone's heard stories about the town's first detective and his amazing disguises.) But sometimes the local lads won't let me in on their plans, in case I snitch. And anytime I'm caught out doing something not quite respectable, people know exactly where to march me back to. So that's what I was thinking about while I stood there, getting another dressing down from our mam.

"You don't know you're born, our Charlie," Mam was saying. "Not so long ago, a boy your age would've been put to work in a factory. Then you'd have had no time for larking about."

"It's hard to have too much fun when every pig in the borough knows your face–." As soon as the word was out of my mouth, I wanted to take it back – but there it was, hanging in the air like a bad smell. I felt hot blood rush into my cheeks and my throat got tight. "Every policeman, I mean–."

Dad looked at me, hard, right in the eye, for a moment, then stood up and walked out. I'd expected a row. The silence felt strange, like he'd sucked all the air out of the room when he'd left.

"Oh, Charlie–," Mam began. I hated how sad she looked. A hot prickling started all over my face and neck. But at the same time I was thinking, *how upset can you be about one little word? When all the lads down town use it, too?* The tingling subsided as I thought about Mam and Dad trying to pen me in like one of Dad's prisoners. It weren't fair. I swallowed down the lump in my throat and headed out into the sunshine. After a while I attempted to whistle – but the tune sounded too jaunty, so I passed through the shadow of St. Margaret's church tower in silence.

I stood in the street a while, kicking a kerbstone until the toe of my boot was scuffed.

"Good afternoon to ye," said a voice.

I swung around. A young man with dark unkempt hair stood across the street, his shirt half unbuttoned and his necktie askew. It was Fin – one of the crowd I'd seen hanging around outside the boarding house. I thought about what our mam had said about bad elements, I did, and about what Dad would do if he caught me down here again. Then I thought about what I'd be going back to if I went home now, and I left off kicking and crossed the street.

"Good afternoon," I said, holding out my hand. I hadn't forgotten my manners.

Fin was a bit dishevelled, maybe, but he was polite enough. Some of his friends were meeting up, he said; would I like to join them? Of course I would!

Spending time with Fin was so different from sitting in the stuffy parlour with my lot. Everyone in Fin's crowd had something interesting to say. Dark brown bottles were passed from hand to hand as the afternoon slipped into evening; in the lamplight, the lads' eyes shone like black pebbles in a stream. One after the other, they stood up to have their say, roughly wiping their mouths on their shirtsleeves. If the group thought Pat or Joe had spoken for too long – well Pat or Joe would be shoved aside so that Jim or Col could take his turn.

I'll be honest, I felt a little shy. But Fin's friends drew me into their conversation: "Don't you agree, Charlie?"

"Would you credit that, now, Charlie?"

When Fin stood up to tell a wild story, the other lads hooted and shouted, "It were not so!" but I could see in their eyes that they loved Fin's tall tales as much as I did. I sat in silence, just listening. I weren't sure what they'd make of me being the son of a sergeant – I mean, the way Fin told it, if you're down in the gutter you can bet there's a copper looking over your shoulder, blocking your view of the sun. But there's a lot of good bobbies: I've known some of 'em all my life. Eventually I had to say something so I mumbled my confession:

"My … erm … my dad's a bobby."

"Why, then, Charlie," said Fin, clapping me on the back, "you must have some grand tales to tell, for sure."

"Tales? Me?"

I felt a bit light-headed then, because I *did* have stories. You hear some strange things around a police station, I can tell you. I began awkwardly, but as the lads drew closer around me my words flowed. I told them how one constable had been caught passed out on the floor: resting after a busy shift, he'd claimed. I told them how another had entertained a lady in the station house late at night when no one else was on duty – and how he'd had his pay docked, because he should have been concentrating on his work. The lads enjoyed that story: they nudged one another, grinning. I was bursting to tell another and I'd saved the best for last. This was something I'd seen with me own eyes, a secret – and every time I thought of it I couldn't help but smile.

Constable Merryweather was supposed to patrol the streets around the Fleur-de-lis, but I knew that – as soon as he could – he'd sneak into an outhouse and spend the night in there, out of the wind and rain. I didn't know how he could stand it, all night in a stinking privy, but Merryweather didn't seem to care. He could get so comfortable that he'd fall right asleep: I'd heard his snoring sometimes, when I'd crept up close. I suppose I should have told Dad, you know, that criminals were safe to roam the streets on old Merryweather's watch, but like I told the lads, then he'd have known I'd been hanging around by the inn again – and I'd have got no thanks for that.

A couple of days after I'd met Fin and his friends, I was still fizzing inside. I'm sure I was walking with a lively step that evening as I headed down Belgrave Gate. I weren't being reckless, mind; I still had to avoid being seen by Dad's men, for one thing, so I was keeping my eyes open. But, as cagey as I was acting, my heart seemed to be soaring somewhere above me, beating loud enough for anyone to hear.

Walking up ahead, I saw a couple of Fin's gang – I recognised Joe – and I rushed to catch up with them. I was just on the point of springing forward and saying hello when I noticed a copper heading toward us, his stave swinging like a great pendulum at his side. The lads must've spotted him too and we all stepped smartly into the shadows, before I could catch their eye – me stuck on one side of a wall and them on the other. I imagined myself as a great criminal, evading arrest; the copper coming down the road was, in my imagination, not just any old constable but the famous Tanky Smith – and he was hunting me down.

As I stood there, trying not to breathe or make any sound, I heard a muted voice from over the wall. It was Joe, I was sure, and I strained my ears to listen.

"Ay, Fin reckons tonight's the night. Some of the boys are out on the streets already, and they're fairly riled up. Let's visit our friendly local innkeeper – and see if we can't knock some sense into him."

There was laughter from their side of the wall, and I stood on tiptoes to hear more.

"It were a grand ruse," Joe continued, "getting the stuff from that copper's kid. He reckons the fat old bluebottle sleeps in the privy behind the pub. Best place for him. So no one's going to raise the alarm when the lads get rowdy."

Copper's kid? My scalp prickled as I listened. What had I started?

"Let's get going. I think all's clear."

"Ay, we wouldn't want to miss the fun."

I heard the two of them walking away and I didn't know what to do. What were they up to? I half made up my mind to go home and spend a dull evening in the parlour. But – what if something really bad were happening? If they wanted Merryweather out of the way, it couldn't be good.

Right, I told myself, time to turn detective. What would Tanky do? I took off my cap and jacket, bundled them up, and pushed them into a crevice. The night was warm enough and maybe I wouldn't be recognised without them. Then I followed Joe and his mate at a distance. One or two other lads – youths I hadn't seen before – joined them as they walked along. One opened his jacket and pulled something from inside. He held it high above his head and then brought it down, hard, in a swinging blow; it was a shillelagh, a cudgel, I saw, before Joe made him hide it away.

"Save that for the chucker-out, if he tries to block our way," I heard Joe say. "He'll be in for a bad thing, if he don't show us some respect."

I'd seen enough to know there would be trouble – trouble for me, sooner or later, whether I got involved or not. I swallowed hard. Dad was going to kill me. I left the road and scooted through the maze of yards and jittys, going as quickly as I could. Before too long I was behind the Fleur-de-lis, looking out for Constable Merryweather.

"Oi! Master Tarratt!"

I jumped about a foot in the air. Old Merryweather was light on his feet, for such a hefty fellow. But I was relieved to see him.

"Hello, Constable Merryweather," I stuttered. "Listen, erm, there's going to be trouble–."

"You're not wrong there, young man. When your father hears you've been down here–."

"Please!" I must have sounded upset, because he stopped just as he was getting going. "Please – there's going to be some kind of barney. The lads... well, some lads... they've been drinking... they've got weapons..." In halting sentences, I told him as much as I dared.

"You stay put," he said, pressing his top hat more firmly onto his head. "I mean it – get yourself out of sight, and not a peep until I come back. I'll get a message to the station; they'll send help – in case things get ugly."

I didn't want to think about things getting ugly.

I watched Merryweather bowl across the courtyard; his blue

coattails trailed out behind him and I would've laughed if my innards hadn't been tied in knots. One thing I did know: I was not spending the night by the latrines – not even part of the night. As soon as Merryweather was out of sight I slipped along to Bread Street. I wouldn't say the air was fresh, but it was fresher and I breathed a little more easily.

Not for long. Peering around the corner, I saw a crowd of young men pour into Belgrave Gate – twenty of them, maybe thirty. Their shouts echoed off the walls of the terraced houses. They banged on windows and doors, and swung sticks and sickles above their heads. Then a cry went up, a brick was hurled, and suddenly everything was in motion.

Looking around, I saw what they had seen: four men in blue at the other end of the street. Outnumbered as they were, they walked steadily towards the heaving mass. There was Dad; I could see he was issuing instructions, although I couldn't hear his words. I wanted to shout out, to tell him to go back – but my throat had closed.

When I saw one of the bobbies crumple under a blow from a shillelagh, everything seemed to go into slow motion and I had plenty of time to think about what I'd done. How could I have been so stupid, blabbing my secret like that? Constable Wright – Fred, as our dad called him – raised a hand part-way to his head and sank gracefully to the ground. His top hat had been knocked forward, low on his brow. I had time to see that he looked slightly puzzled. Behind him, his attacker raised his club again and looked around for another victim.

Dad and the others brandished their own staves, but they were soon surrounded on all sides. I edged closer and was relieved to see Dad's face above the crowd. He was half a head taller than most of the lads in the rabble. But as I watched, he suddenly reeled backwards. I didn't see the rock that hit him; I just saw his white face turn scarlet. Half blinded, he staggered sideways. No! I pushed my way through the jostling crowd and caught him by the arm. In the crush we were pushed and shoved on all sides. Dad couldn't see anything, I think, and all I could see were patched elbows as they swung near my face. I put my head down and ran, crab-like, hunched over, pulling our dad along behind. A hail of stones fell around us.

I saw a gap at the edge of the crowd and shoved Dad, hard. He grabbed me as he stumbled, then pulled me clean over with him. We rolled over on the cobbles, once, twice, then came to a stop in the reeking gutter as we hit the kerb. I felt no pain, just numbness. Dad groaned and half sat up, wiping blood from his forehead.

There was a distant rattling, and some of the rioters hooted. Then more rattling, louder and closer. I lifted my head.

"Dad, Dad, it's your mates!" Coppers were charging up the street in pairs, waving nightsticks and whirling heavy rattles. The rioters slung a few beer bottles in their direction, sang a few bars of a rude song, then melted away.

Dad tried to straighten his jacket, and winced. He shook his head, just a fraction, as he ran a finger over the dented silver buttons. Then his eyes widened and he reached out to touch my shirt: on the dark fabric, a darker stain was spreading. Blood? My heart gave one big 'glug' as I shifted my shirt to peer inside. Then I smiled – and grimaced – and grinned, holding out my bloody hand.

"Pig," I said.

"Pig?" asked Dad.

He glanced along the gutter where we sat, at the dark liquid spreading stickily around us and the lumps of grey-brown offal that lay like silent tongues. A smile spread across his face, and then he was laughing like I'd never seen him laugh before. He scooped me towards him and we stood up together, bruised but intact. He was still laughing when we reached his men, who were patching up Constable Wright.

"Let's not mention any of this to your mam, eh?" he said and winked.

Maharajah: the Elephant who Walked to Manchester

ANNA MAINWARING

I SIT WITH ONE LEG on either side of a wobbly gate, staring at the dusty road. A dark swarm of swallows dart, turn and swoop in the late spring evening above me. Sunlight has turned the hills to gold but discontent means that I cannot see their beauty today. Below is the village in which I have lived quietly for fourteen years. There is one church, two hundred houses, a small school, a meagre handful of shops and a hotel, mostly untroubled by custom, which stands opposite the vicarage where I live.

As the birds above fly down the valley, I think about what they will see as they go. First the smoky smudge of Manchester, all factories, chimneys and – according to Mother – sin. But at least as Jane our cook says, "There's allus summat to see." Then they might fly south to London, capital of the empire, where Queen Victoria, Empress of India, sits on her throne. I've never seen a queen. I don't think I've ever seen anything that matters. I wonder if I ever will.

"Are they coming yet?" asks my younger brother William who sits on the verge at my feet. He holds in his hand a small, battered but much loved wooden elephant which has today been liberated from Noah's Ark to accompany us as we wait.

So far we have seen the post carriage, four carts and Mr Tranter, the local wool merchant on his fat horse, who chats warmly to William. But his eyes take in my lack of hat, my unbraided hair, the way my legs straddle the gate. Not for the first time I know that a telling off will await me when Mother hears of this.

"I've told you," a note of irritation creeps in, "there's nothing to see." I bite my lip, "Maybe they're not coming tonight. Maybe they're not coming at all."

As soon as the words leave my lips, I feel ashamed as tears begin to tumble down his fat cheeks.

I jump down from my vantage point and give him a hug.

"But they left Kendal yesterday, the newspaper said," William persists, "so they should arrive here tonight." In his other hand is the now dogged rectangle of paper he regards as an Oracle. "Tell me the story of the elephant again, Clara," he begs.

"If I must," I say, "Maharajah was born in India, where monkeys live in every tree and fakirs are as common as beggars and they can steal your soul as quick as look at you. When he was a baby, his mother died and he was taken in and sold to a zoo in Scotland. Imagine how he must have cried on that long journey from the heat of India to the dark nights and short days of the north."

"I think I might cry, if that were me," William says sadly.

I smile and continue my story, "Well, after a few years of this, Maharajah was sold again and this time his home is to be..."

"Manchester!" cries William, "And Father says that one day we might go to the zoo at Belle Vue to see him."

"Yes," I agree, "but the story is not over yet is it? When the zoo keeper took Maharajah to the station to put him upon the train to Manchester, Maharajah just took one look at the little dark carriage that they wanted him to go into and said (in elephant language) 'I'd really rather not, Sir, if it's all the same to you.' And with that he..."

William chimes in and finishes the story, "...lifted up both big feet and smashed the carriage to pieces!" His face is now glowing as he thinks of the elephant running amok at a busy station. I feel sad as I think of Maharajah's fear of the steam, the noise and the people. What right did anyone have to sell him as if he was a bale of cotton?

"And then..." William insists.

"And then... the keeper said, 'Maharajah must go to Manchester. But if he won't go on a train and we can't go on a boat, then we must walk - we must walk all the way to Manchester.'"

"And he's going to come through our village," William calls triumphantly. "An elephant, a real elephant all the way from India, and we're going to see him!"

"But not tonight," a deep familiar voice says.

"Father," William runs towards the tall figure that stands a few feet away from us, clad in his usual dark clothes with a collar of white. Father hugs him close and ruffles his fair hair.

"Your mother has sent me to bring you home. I fear that Maharajah will not be visiting tonight." I try to protest but my father holds up his hand.

"Enough, Clara, we have indulged you in your whim but now it is time for prayers and bed."

He looks at me with his stern eyes that brook no argument.

"Clara, you're not wearing a hat. I hope you have not made a spectacle of yourself this afternoon. People look at you and judge me." He pauses as he looked at me sadly. "Decorum, Clara, decorum."

Inside, I burn to say so many things. But experience has taught

me that to fight with my father ends with my hand burning with the pain from a ruler and my heart on fire with shame. Because my father is a vicar, I must be like a doll. Always pretty, always smiling, always silent.

So my father and William walk home hand in hand, with me walking five paces behind. I kick a stone in anger, it flies up and narrowly misses my father's leg, landing in a puff of dust just in front of him. I brace myself as he turns around. But to my surprise, his face is not angry as I expect but rather sad.

"I know you are disappointed, Clara," he says. "But the Lord does not always give us what we want." I have heard this all my life and always thought it meant only for me. But now, looking at my father's face, carved with lines of care from long days and late nights tending for his parishioners, I consider for the first time if he is really talking about himself.

Father stands still for a moment, his eyes focused on the distant road, just as William and I have all afternoon. "I wonder..." he muses.

"What, Father?" Will asks.

My father smiles his wintry smile. "Nothing, boy, nothing but nonsense and moonshine. Now time for bed and prayers."

An hour later I am in bed, though sleep is far from me. Shadows are deepening in the corners of the nursery. But I have a precious candle. Mother took one look at my face when I came in and said I could read tonight until the candle burns down. William, now just a lump under his blanket, is snoring. But I see his hand, jutting out from under the covering. The wooden elephant still held fast in his grasp.

I pull from under my pillow my hidden copy of 'Arabian Nights'. The candle is burning brightly. Without wasting any time,

I turn to my favourite tale and fall into another world that's full of magic, wonder and light.

All too quickly, the flame hisses and dies as it drowns in a pool of wax. I put my book back under my pillow and shiver as I climb out of bed and kneel on the wooden floor.

"Dear Lord," I say, "I'm sorry I'm such a bad daughter. I'm sorry my hair got untidy. I know I'm being a baby about wanting to see the elephant, but I'm fourteen and nothing really has ever happened to me. It must be nice to be you, you can see everything from up there. But down here, the view is very small." I take a deep breath. "So please Lord, if it's not too much trouble, could you make sure that William and I see Maharajah?"

All is still in the room, save for William's thick breathing. I strain my eyes and ears for some sign that He has heard me. It is cold now and my knees are starting to hurt. I climb back into bed and close my eyes. In my head, I see the long road that leads north to Kendal. It is dark now and lit only by stars. But the darkness is moving. A large shadow shambles along.

I try to sleep but my mind is too full of dreams and my heart is too full of pain. And so, in the darkness, I imagine that I'm telling William stories and he and I sit close while I tell him of Scheherazade, Ali Baba and the Roc. Half wakeful, half sleepy, my mind becomes a tangle of thoughts and pictures.

And then I sit bolt upright in bed. There's a noise from outside.

Moonlight, bright as milk, pours over my pillow. I open the window and let the cold breeze seep around me. Do I wake or do I dream?

Through the budding leaves of the copper beech tree in the paddock, the perfect silver circle of the moon burns against the sky. I cup my hand and gaze up at it. I wonder what our world looks like from there. I'd like to fly to the moon when it has waned to a crescent. I would sit on the curve and swing among the stars, grabbing at comets as they pass by and drinking from the Milky Way.

Then something startles me.

The darkness moves below under the tree. I strain my eyes to see what is there, shuffling in the dark.

Whatever it is, it is large.

Whatever it is, it is not normally there.

My hearts pounds in my chest.

Should I cry out? The street between the paddock gate and the hotel is quiet. Could a cow have got loose and found its way in?

Whatever it is, it snuffles.

It moves forward from beneath the branches of the tree and then I see it. I see *him*.

Dark liquid eyes look up at me.

"Thank you, Lord," I repeat over and over again. And then I quickly make my way to William's bed. He protests as I gently shake him awake and I put a finger to his lips.

"I've got a surprise for you," I whisper. "Come with me."

Rubbing his eyes, he puts his small hand in mine and follows me out of our bedroom, across the landing and down the stairs. By now his eyes are large with concern. "Will Father be cross with us?" he mouths to me.

"Only if he finds out," I mouth back.

But despite my words, I find my hands sweating as I stand on the stool from the kitchen. I ease back the bolts that fasten the door from the inside. Fortunately, Jane has oiled them recently and they slide back easily. Carefully, I push the door open and William and I walk out into the moonlit night.

We follow the path that leads from the kitchen garden to the front of the house and then to the paddock opposite the hotel.

Where the beech tree stands dark in the moonlight.

And under the tree, we can see as clear as if it were daylight, there is an elephant. The Lord heard me and He has, in his infinite goodness, answered my prayers.

William's eyes shine in the night. "Is it him?" he whispers. "Is it Maharajah?"

The elephant takes a step towards us, his long trunk, as crinkled as crepe paper, feeling the air in front of him. His back almost touches the lowest branches of the tree. Even if I stood on my tip toes, I would not be able to touch it. His skin is as creased as the leather that covers the books in my father's study but unlike the books, it is covered in fine hairs. His eyes are dark and full of feeling.

I put my hand out towards his trunk. Softly, the tip of it dances around my fingers. I can feel his hot breath on my skin. "Come, William," I say, "put out your hand too." So William edges out from behind me.

"Hello, Maharajah," he says. And Maharajah nods his large head, his tusks gleaming bone white, his trunk now snaking forward to snuffle William's hand. William takes hold of it and gently moves it up and down.

"How do you do?" William says and I smile at his manners. "I don't know if you speak English, or whether you speak like a heathen, but welcome to our small town."

Maharajah moves forward slightly and now his trunk feels William's head, breathing on his face. I stand next to him and then he touches my hair, the dark strands blow gently from the wind of his breath.

"How can this have happened?" says William. "Is it magic?"

"I asked God last night," I say.

"Thank you God," Williams calls, his face upturned to the sky.

"Thank you, Clara," he says and kisses me.

And then he walks slowly round Maharajah, his hand trailing over the elephant's rough skin. I see his eyes drinking in every aspect of the creature, his thick legs, his strange horn-like toes and his tail that narrows to a skein of wispy hair. His ears are the same shape as Africa, one the right way, one as if seen in a mirror.

As William comes round, his hand now runs down the ivory of Maharajah's tusk, touches the dull point of the end and then comes back to the metal bar that runs between his tusks where a chain leads to the tree. Even a mighty beast such as this is not free.

"Why do you think they put this on him?" William asks. "Do you think it hurts him?"

"I don't know," I reply.

"Oh well," William says cheerfully, "I'll ask him." With that, he sits down cross legged, his nightgown making him look like a ghost. And then Maharajah kneels down, his huge legs creaking like trees.

As the stars slowly wheel above us, William's voice rises and falls like a stream as he pours out his heart to our silent visitor. When his voice falls silent, as sleep finally claims him, he snuggles into the side of the elephant. And Maharajah wraps his trunk around him.

And then I begin to speak and all my hopes and dreams tumble out into the moonlight. Then I too rest my heavy head against his warm bulk as I slide into a kaleidoscope of dreams where two children ride on the back of a white elephant, flying through the stars and, finally, alighting on the dusty surface to dance upon the moon.

"Good morning, children." A deep voice tears me from sleep. I wake to realise that I am frozen to my core. I leap to my feet, my teeth chattering.

"Father, it was me. I opened the door and I bought William out here. Be angry with me but don't be angry with him."

I stare at my father's impassive face, trying to see his reaction to the scene in front of him. It is no dream. There is an elephant in the garden, William still wrapped in his trunk, tucked close to its side.

"That is a sight I never thought to see," Father says thoughtfully. He bends down to pat William on the head.

"He is a fine creature. And apparently gentle."

"I asked God last night for Maharajah to come and then he did," I said.

A rare smile lights up my father's face. "Then I am the Lord's agent. When I returned from visiting Widow Franklin, I passed the hotel. The beast had just arrived and the stables were too small for him. They were looking for alternative lodgings for our pachyderm friend and I thought of you two and offered our paddock."

I hug my father with all my strenght. "Thank you, Papa."

He holds me close for a few precious seconds. "Now, go in and get dressed. Then we'll see about getting you and our visitor some breakfast."

Light as a bird, I fly back in the house and make myself respectable. I braid my hair with fingers as fast as my heartbeat. When I return, Father is, deep in conversation with a gentleman whose face is lined and tanned by travel, as Maharajah munches on a bale of hay.

"Clara, may I introduce you to Mr Lorenzo Lawrence, Maharajah's keeper." Mr Lawrence sounds more Scottish than his name suggests. As the men chat, I sit and stroke Maharajah's trunk and stare into his eyes. He stares back. "Remember the moon," I whisper and his trunk dances round my head and tickles my face.

"Time for us to move on," Mr Lawrence says and he

clicks with his tongue, then taps Maharajah with his cane. At the command, the huge elephant lumbers to his feet. "We must be in Manchester today. The press will be waiting for us at four o'clock. Just in time to make the late editions." He strokes the elephant's trunk affectionately and Maharajah snickers back at him.

With one final touch of the hat, Mr Lawrence says goodbye to us and starts to walk down the road. People begin to gather, windows open as all hang out to see them pass.

William, suddenly awake, runs down the street after them.

"Goodbye Maharajah," he calls, waving his small wooden elephant after him, "I'll never forget you."

Father walks swiftly after William, making sure he does not get lost in the crowd.

But I stay where I am.

I see Maharajah pace down the street, down the road to smoky Manchester where the crowds are waiting for him.

But in my mind as he fades into dust I see two children, one with dark hair, one with fair, seated high on the back of an elephant that flies among the stars.

The John Library

SHERRY ASHWORTH

October 5th, 1899

BECAUSE THE WIND BLEW THE GENTLEMAN'S HAT OFF, Johnny was able to sneak inside. The gentlemen and even the lady had stepped away from the entrance to watch the bowler hat dance into the middle of Deansgate and get crushed by a dray horse. But Johnny didn't see any of that. As quick as thought he was inside, hurtling up the grand staircase, and then found himself in pitch darkness.

Johnny didn't mind the darkness. In fact, it suited him. As far as he was concerned, it couldn't be dark enough. He wanted to be where *they* couldn't find him. He wanted to be where he couldn't even find himself, his shame was so great. And no one at all would think of looking for him here, in the new, huge, pink building on Deansgate.

Gradually his eyes became accustomed to the lack of light. He could see dark lines that he guessed were pillars, and more staircases. He had never been in such a big building in the whole of his life. It bewildered him. He was used to the streets of Manchester, to the hubbub of Shudehill market, to the throngs on Deansgate, but the solemn silence and vast dark spaces of this building made him shiver.

And then the lights came on.

Johnny was terrified. It was magic – it had to be! For no one had been to turn the gas lamps on, and yet a soft illumination spread over the landing, and he could see staircases to either side of him, a vaulted ceiling, and fluted pillars. His heart pounding, he careered up the nearest staircase, turned a corner and found himself in a church-like room with alcoves full of books. Hundreds and thousands of books. He saw a smaller, spiral staircase, wreathed in shadows, and darted up it. He slowed down as he reached a turn, and sat for a while to give his pulse a chance to slow, to take stock of what he'd done and think about where he was.

He thought he'd once heard someone say this building was a library, which is what you called a building full of books. It was the first library he had been in, and the last place *they* would think of looking for him. If he could hide here for a day or two, his pursuers would lose his trail, and he could escape and go – go where? But what would he do for food and water? Johnny made fists of his hands and knuckled his eyes. It stopped him crying.

Did he hear something? Was it voices? Yes – and footsteps too. He was still as a stone, trying to catch what words he could.

"Are you sure, Ma'am?"

"Perfectly sure, Mr Champneys."

"We will wait for you below."

"Thank you."

The conversation ceased. Had they all gone? Johnny feared discovery, and so he sneaked higher up the staircase, until it came to an end. He was in a gallery overlooking the main library. Overcome by curiosity, he crept to the wooden balustrade, crouched down next to a table, and peered between two mahogany bars and looked down. Although lit, the library was still dim, and it took him some time to find the lady, who was standing in the centre of the main aisle looking around her.

She was a very tall lady, in a dark bonnet, with a black coat over a long, satiny skirt. Johnny could not tell how old she was. The old people he knew were bent and wrinkled and not nice to look at. But this lady wasn't young neither.

"John!" she said.

Johnny was so shocked to hear his name that his whole frame convulsed. He knocked against the table next to him, and the lady looked up.

"Who's there?" she cried, with alarm.

Johnny stayed stock still, hoping the lady would think she had imagined the noise. A moment later she called, "Come down. I can see you."

This was the end. It was all over. She would take him to the police for intruding and they would lock him up. *They* would find him, and worse would follow. All the heart went out of him. Johnny shuffled over to the spiral staircase and slowly made his way down.

Enriqueta Rylands took a deep, long breath. The intruder was just a boy, not a thief intent on purloining one of the priceless manuscripts she had acquired. She would reprimand him and take him down to Champneys and the others, for detention. She waited until he appeared from the spiral staircase.

Yes. She was right. He was just a street arab. Barefoot, with trousers that were too long for him, rolled up around his ankles. Both his trousers and jacket were threadbare and ripped in places. She could see a flash of white from his bare leg. His face was smeared with dirt, and his cap was too big for him. It was hard to guess how old he was. Nine? Ten?

He stood there, removed his cap, bent his head in deference and waited for her anger to descend on him.

"What are you doing here?" she asked, sternly.

"Hidin', Ma'am."

"Hiding? From whom?"

"Them as is looking for me, Ma'am."

Enriqueta smiled to herself. "And your name?"

"John, Ma'am. Them as knows me calls me Johnny. Johnny Cropper. Please don't take me to the p'lice, Miss."

"Then tell me a little more about what you're doing here."

Johnny reached down and scratched his leg, straightened himself, cleared his throat, then twisted his cap in his hands.

"Ma'am, I stole summat. But I couldn't 'elp it and it warn't their money anyway. Christ! Is that a ghost?"

Johnny's eyes were transfixed in horror at the spectrally white figure to his left. Enriqueta could not help but smile.

"That is a statue of my husband, John Rylands."

Johnny reached his hand out and gingerly prodded the cold marble.

"Is 'e dead?"

Enriqueta took a breath before she spoke. "He is."

"Who builded that statue of him? You?"

"No – another man called John, as it happens. But I asked him to build it."

"Why?"

"It is right that my husband should be in the library that bears his name."

"The John library?"

"The John Rylands library."

"I heer'd of the Rylands. I knowed folk who works there. In the mills."

"Do you have employment, Johnny?"

The boy hung his head. His heart was bursting. The posh lady had a funny voice, like all the posh people, but she didn't sound angry, and she was a world removed from those who were out to get him. She was like an angel, with a stern face and kind eyes. Even if she was going to turn him in, he thought it would be a relief to tell her his story, like you would tell God when you died.

"I 'ad a job once, Ma'am, yer honour."

"You can call me Mrs Rylands. Come, take a seat."

She walked over to a table, and pulled out a chair. She indicated Johnny should sit there, and she drew up another opposite him. Her skirts rustled as she lowered herself onto it. Johnny could see from the way she sat that her back was bothering her, same as the old folk he knew.

"What's in all the books, Ma'am Mrs Rylands yer honour?"

"Some are about the words of God, others are about travels

and the world we live in."

"Like hymns, Miss? Do they have hymns? *Jesus loves me. This I know; For the Bible tells me so.*"

"Some might have hymns. Where did you learn that hymn, Johnny?"

"Over the road, Miss. At the Mission."

"You've been to the Wood Street School? Johnny, let me know your history. Please."

"It in't a good story, Miss. I used to sell the noos. After school in the morning, I'd go t' noosepaper office and get the papers. Then I'd stand on mi corner and call out for folk to buy 'em. I have to make a shillin' a day. Else she'll kill me."

"Who will kill you?"

"Mi mam. She says, bring me a shillin' home. She needs it for the gin. When I come 'ome I gives her the money and she goes out and leaves me with the littluns. There was four of us but Nellie died last winter. If it weren't for the littluns I'd scarper."

"How old are you, Johnny?"

"Ten, Miss. How old are you?"

Enriqueta Rylands paused, unsure how to answer the question.

"Quite old," she said.

"I thought so," Johnny continued. "So as I was sayin', I sold the noos, and then one day the wind was blowin' hard, and took all mi papers and they landed in the mud. So I took 'em and washed 'em at the pump, but that weren't a good idea. They turned into a mush, so I couldn't sell 'em. I was afeerd I wouldn't have my shillin'.

"Then these lads I know, they come along, and says not to worry, and they was laughin' and they said they'd show me how to get some money. I thought they was going to take me begging, honest, Miss. But they takes me along to a ware'us, and says to me to keep a lookout. One of 'em gets in through a winder and the others follow. I waits but no one comes. Then they come out with a bundle, and gives me my shillin'. I knowed that was wrong, Miss Rylands.

"Then when I gets home, mi mam, she's already been at the gin. And she throwed a dish at me – it caught me eye and made it bleed. And the littluns set up an unholy racket. So I ran off and spent the night in Shudehill under a barrow. The next morning, I goes to the Mission in Wood Street as I en't had anything to eat."

"That was a wise thing to do," said Mrs Rylands.

"Oh, Miss, I had to – I were clemmed wi' hunger. And I'd heerd tell of the breakfasts at the Mission. I didn't have a token like the other lads but they gives me coffee, bread and butter, and tells me to come back for dinner. It's reet good there, Miss. You should go. You line up with your spoon, and bang it on the table, then you sing the hymns, and they gives you bread and soup. Proper soup with peas and bacon. And then a gennleman says I could come again. And he might give me some learning and help me get a job. Is this library for learning, Miss?"

Mrs Rylands looked around her. "Yes. I hope people like you will come here and discover how to make the best of yourselves. It's what my husband would have wanted."

"Did 'e build the library, same as the mills?"

"No. But Mr Rylands loved books and I hope he would be proud to know I have done this in his name."

"So you built the library, Miss? But beg my pardon, you're a lady! Ladies don't do anything 'cept go to the thee-atre."

"Not all ladies are the same. But tell me more. If you attended the Wood Street Boys' School, why are you hiding here?"

"I did, Miss Rylands. I went there and learned me letters good. And me numbers – I was quick at numbers. So the gennleman there, he got me a position. I was the boy in the plumber's shop. It were reet good, Miss. The plumber said he would 'prentice me.

"Then one day he leaves me in the shop to go to Ancoats for some pipes. And those lads came in, same as before. I knowed them well. They called me a toff, and one of them, he spits on the counter, and I goes to a rubbin' and cleanin' and they laugh and spits some more. Soon, one of 'em says they need me that night, and I says no. Till he picks up a tap from the counter and puts it in his pocket and runs. I shout, you can't do that, and I runs after him, and I left the shop open Miss. That were wrong. I looks all around, and I can't see the lads anywhere. Then one jumps out on me and pins me to the floor, and says they'll give me the tap back in the morning if I meets them that night.

"Miss, I knowed I shouldn't have. Miss, I know. But I thought if I got the tap back, no harm would be done. So I meets them, and this time they sends me in through a 'aberdasher's window, wi' me being small. They tell me to take the money from below the counter. And I did it. I gets outside and asks for the tap back. And they just laugh and carry on smokin'. They say I'm lucky to be in one piece, and to hand over the cash.

"So I run, Miss. I can run fast, wi' me being small. They goes after me but I dash into a courtyard and shimmy up the wall at the back, and dive down and land in a dustbin. I pull all the rubbish over me and wait. Christ, it stunk! But it all goes quiet, and dark. And when I pop my head out, it's night, too late to go home, and I walk the streets and wait for the morning to wash at the pump. And all day I been hiding from them. I still got the money. But the plumber won't have me back, not now."

"You should go back to the Mission, Johnny."

"Miss, I were going to. That's why I'm here, Miss. But in the end, I couldn't. That gennleman, he could never forgive a wretch like me, Miss. He gave me a chance and I threw it away. I ain't never going back there, not never. I'm too ashamed, Miss."

"No, Johnny. I know the gentleman, and he is a Christian. He will forgive you. You must gather your courage and –,"

"Miss, why are you in the library all by yourself in the night? Are you gonna do a bit of reading?"

"No. Tomorrow the library will be inaugurated – that means, opened officially. There will be a ceremony, and music, and lots of important people, and I wanted to be here alone first."

"You want to think about your husband, Miss."

Enriqueta Rylands looked at the boy, surprised. "I do."

"Was 'e good to you?"

"Very good indeed. Had he lived, tomorrow would have been our wedding anniversary."

"Congratulations, Miss Rylands."

"How I wish we could have just been alone together in Longford Hall. But instead tomorrow I shall be here, and there shall be speeches and newspaper men and a fuss. I do not like a fuss."

"Me, I don't like a fuss neither."

"I have no desire to be in the limelight. I only want to do good for its own sake. Not for the honours and accolades. The greatest blessing is a quiet life."

"It is indeed, Miss."

"Perhaps, tomorrow, I shall send my brother to give my excuses. He can stand in my place. I have no wish to be celebrated. The library exists for the good of God, the people and is in memory of my husband. I should not be there."

"Miss Rylands, you're shy. You got the collywobbles."

"I do not like being the centre of public attention."

"Oh, Miss. You're a coward you are! If you built this library then you got to be there when it opens. It in't fair otherwise."

"No, Johnny. I have made up my mind. I will not attend the inauguration."

"But Miss you got to!"

Enriqueta shook her head. "Many people think that a lady should not have a public position. They intend to give me the freedom of the City of Manchester. How can I accept that?"

"The freedom, Miss! That's the best thing you could have. You deserve it!"

"I will decline, I think."

Enriqueta glanced quickly at the boy's face. It was etched with disappointment.

"But there is one thing that might change my mind."

"What's that?"

"If you had the courage to go back to the Mission, then I think I might find the courage to attend the inauguration tomorrow."

Johnny was silent for a while. "But it's different. I done a bad thing. I stoled. You done a good thing."

"It makes no difference. As long as each of us does the best we can, God will judge. If your heart is good, you have done nothing of which you should be ashamed."

That was when both heard the approach of footsteps. Two gentlemen and a man in livery entered the library.

"You have been a long time, Mrs Rylands, and we thought –,"

"What on earth is this vagabond doing here?"

"Shall we call the police?"

"That will not be necessary. Johnny was on his way to the Mission, and I invited him here to view the library. I hope one day when he has completed his education, he will read here. Johnny, are you ready to go the back to the Mission?"

"Mrs Rylands, I am. Are you going to the opening thing tomorrow?"

"Indeed I am."

Both rose, and Johnny slid his hand into the cool palm of Mrs Rylands.

A gentleman muttered, "I didn't see him come in here."

Another said, "What's Mrs Rylands up to now?"

"Enough," said Mrs Rylands. "Once we are gone, you can lock the building. Mr Champneys, arrange for my carriage to collect me from the Wood Street Mission."

She looked up at the statue of her husband, and the flickering electric lights seemed, just for a moment, to suggest a smile playing on his lips.

The Fall

ALISON PADLEY-WOODS

TED WAS DOUBLED OVER, resting his hands on his knees and taking great gulps of air as he looked up. His blond fringe fell across his face and his freckled cheeks, now puce and shiny from running, opened into a huge dimpled grin displaying a chipped front tooth from an earlier fall.

Ted loved a good race, but he wasn't too bothered about losing, not today. It was his first time in the country and nothing was going to spoil that. He straightened up and brushed his fringe off his sticky forehead as he looked down at his new companions.

"You set off before me. I never heard you say go."

Bob and Charlie were sprawled beside the chestnut tree that overlooked the lake and were still catching their breath, as they glanced at each other and smirked. They'd been evacuees at Tatton Park for almost a month and felt quite the old timers as they lay back on the fallen leaves and looked up into the open sky.

It was October 1940 and each day brought fresh warnings of air strikes. Today, for the time being at least, the skies were at peace and the only thing the boys could hear from above was the gentle hum of the training planes heading towards the park.

Ted yanked his heavy sweater over his head and knotted it around his waist. He'd arrived only yesterday, straight out of Manchester and his clothes still smelled of the smoke in the city, only now there was a good dose of sweat too. His mum had waited on the platform to wave him off and when the train had pulled away, he'd felt the wrench. She'd been subdued, quiet all morning, but he knew she was worrying about his dad – gone six months now without any word.

Ted had pushed that thought from his mind, as he'd squashed himself into the stuffy carriage. It had been crammed with kids, all labelled and carrying gas masks and bags like him and so, he'd stood, hanging onto an overhead railing the whole way to Knutsford. Now, standing beneath the boughs of the tree, he drew in the fresh air and looked out across the lake. There were deer grazing on the other side.

Ted thought back to his mum. Only last week the suffocating smog had lain over them. Then, the air raids had started. At first, Ted hadn't been too worried, not knowing what to expect, but when he'd seen the aftermath, the Palace Theatre bombed and the streets lying in dust and rubble, he'd been scared.

"Have you seen over there," said Bob, "those guys with parachutes, doing training jumps, landing like birds. Have you ever seen anything so amazing?"

Ted looked up. He'd never seen a parachute before.

"What if one gets stuck in a tree?"

"Dunt think that happens much, but if one does get himself in a tangle, maybe you can climb up and cut 'im out!"

Bob was grinning at him, but Ted couldn't take his eyes off the parachutes; the canopies were stretched, full like balloons, floating down until they landed and scrunched into nothing.

"Wouldn't yer love to try it?"

"No way!" said Ted. "I'm scared of heights. Broke my arm falling from a ladder last year; chipped my tooth too." He smiled again, as if to show it off.

"You won't fancy climbing this tree with us then?" said Charlie jumping up and hooking his leg over a branch.

Ted wished he hadn't been so honest, they'd think he was sissy now.

"Suppose I could try."

He reached up and scrambled onto the lowest rung.

"Dare everyone to climb to the top."

Bob was halfway already when he said that and Ted watched, as he and Charlie hauled themselves up, branch after branch, until their heads poked out of the amber leaves. He could barely see them.

"Great camouflage, but I'll stay here, if it's all the same."

"The view from the top's amazing! You can see the planes flying in," called Bob. "Sure you won't come up?"

Ted was gazing across the lake again. He could see the grand mansion through the trees and the deer had just begun to wade across the glistening water.

"Pretty good down here," he began when a tooting noise drowned his voice. The boys turned.

"Lord Egerton!" cried Bob. "Let's race him."

Ted had just recovered from the first round, but the sight of the gleaming car had him running like billyo back through the long grass. The driver gave them a wave as they got close and Ted was there just in time to get a good look as it rolled by. The green paintwork shone in the sun and he could see the name Benz on the back just above the number plate M1.

"Posh intit," smiled Bob as he caught Ted up. "Matron says the M's for Maurice, that's 'is Lordship's name. He lives up at the mansion."

Ted listened to the crunch of its wheels fade into the distance as it disappeared up the gravel drive.

"Be amazing to have a ride, wouldn't it?"

Charlie wasn't listening. He was looking into the sky again at a plane circling the drop zone.

"Let's go to the airfield at Ringway? We went last week dint we Bob? You can see the planes take off. You won't believe it, Ted."

It seemed like a good idea and so the boys set out, chasing through the trees the whole way there. As they approached, a plane was racing down the runway, engine roaring ready for lift off.

"A Whitley bomber!" said Charlie, like he was an expert.

"Shhh!" said Bob. He was watching someone close to the other side of the fence.

"That's the guy we saw last time," he whispered. "We thought he was acting strange, looking a bit shifty."

"He told us to bugger off," said Charlie grinning.

"Did he?"

"Let's spy on 'im, see what he's up to?" said Bob.

"What was he up to las' time?"

"Dunno really. Taking boxes onto a plane, looking over his shoulder all the time, like it was top secret."

Ted didn't think that was so strange, but decided to join in. The man was about his dad's height, but with darker hair and stockier too. He was wearing a belted khaki jacket and matching baggy trousers and he was carrying boxes into the plane.

"What d'ya think he's loading. Ammo? Bombs?" said Bob.

"Parachutes maybe?" Ted wasn't too bothered.

"Why's he keep looking behind then?"

"Dunno!"

They spied on him for some time through slits in the fence.

"Dare someone to sneak over and see what's in the boxes," said Bob.

Ted and Charlie didn't volunteer.

"C'mon! I reckon it's Ted's turn. Us two climbed the tree dint we Charlie."

Ted wasn't sure. He didn't want any trouble on his first day, but he wanted to keep in with his new friends.

"We'll keep look out. If anyone comes we'll do this." Charlie cupped his hands around his mouth and made a long, low, hooting sound like an owl.

"One hoot and all's fine. Two hoots mean leg it." It wasn't far to the plane and the man had disappeared into a hut further away.

"OK. I'll do it."

Ted didn't waste any time then, and quickly hoisted himself over the fence, balancing carefully on top, just long enough to check if the coast was clear.

"Remember, listen out for the hoots," said Charlie.

Ted jumped down on the soft grass and for a moment stood still. Everything was dead quiet; the men must be on a break, or something. Ted took his chance and made towards a short ladder that leaned against the side of the plane. It was just beneath a door that was propped open and Ted paused again at the bottom, checking around and catching a strong whiff of engine oil, soon lost in the breeze.

There was still no sign of anyone and so, Ted climbed gingerly up to the main fuselage, hearing only the scrape of his boots against the metal rungs, as he gripped the ladder tightly. Luckily it wasn't too high and at the top, he glanced down. Glinting back at him was a shiny black puddle on the tarmac beneath one of the engines – a pool of water, oil maybe?

Ted didn't think much about it and stepped inside. It was stuffy and cramped in there, musty too. Six small seats were dotted around and there was a big pile at one end, covered by a peeling tarpaulin. Ted pulled it aside. The boxes! There they were, each labelled No.11 SAS.

Ted wondered if SAS referred to some kind of special battalion, something to ask the others later. Right now his mind kept reverting to the time. He'd only been in there a few moments, but he hated not being able to see what was happening outside.

He was hot and sticky and thinking about re-joining the others when he heard a long low hoot. Ted stood stock-still and listened, but a second hoot didn't come. He sighed. He'd got this far. He could probably prize a lid off a box if he tried and he didn't want to return with nothing to tell.

A toolbox lay open in the corner and Ted quickly found a screwdriver, jarred it under the metal lid and pushed. Nothing budged. Beads of sweat formed across his brow and he was breathing heavily. Still, he wasn't quite ready to give up and so, he tried again.

This time he jammed the metal edge under the lip with greater force. He was using both hands, but his palms were sweaty and as he pushed, the screwdriver slipped. It thumped down, clattering against the metal floor, the noise reverberating around the plane, just as Bob did two long low hoots. Ted only heard the second one.

He grabbed the screwdriver for a last go, thinking it would be his final push, but it was useless and he was just about to give in when he heard a man laughing, then voices. Ted's heart sprung into gear. What could he do? If he legged it, they'd see him, catch him maybe. Then, what?

The voices were getting louder. Ted looked down at the gap between the boxes. He could squeeze in, hide and then sneak out later. It seemed the best option and so as quick as he could, he squashed himself between the metal sides and pulled the damp tarpaulin back over.

The dank musty smell was overpowering and Ted found it hard to breathe as he listened to the men. Their voices had got clearer, then, came the scrape of their boots on the steps. Ted's stomach reeled. He wondered why he'd got himself into this and hoped with all his heart that they'd just dump something and leave.

"Right lads. We're flying straight over the park ready for the drop zone at 3.30pm."

Ted's body was sweating. The smell was making him feel sick and he knew he should come clean while he still could. A silent clock ticked inside him, he was running out of time. He had to do something. Suddenly, a loud rasping noise pierced his ears; it was the metal door sliding down and slamming shut. Next came a buzzing, a whirring of propellers and a jolt, as the engines fired up. It was too late.

"Prepare for take-off."

Why had he done the dare? He wasn't even bothered about what was in the boxes and he was burning up. He badly needed air and the thought of taking off and leaving solid ground was terrifying. Why hadn't Bob and Charlie warned him?

The plane moved slowly at first, bumping gently up and down. Then, the pounding of the wheels against the runway got faster, as the engines screamed into action. Ted desperately wanted to cover his ears, but he couldn't move. The noise was terrific. Everything seemed to accelerate at once and just when he thought the plane might explode, there came a surge. The bumps stopped. Ted's stomach lurched and the plane lifted at such a sharp angle that for a while, he was thankful for being wedged in, fearing he might otherwise roll out of his hiding place.

What could he do? His ears popped, his legs were numb from crouching down and his left arm tingled with pins and needles. He hadn't found out what was in the boxes. If the men didn't need what was inside, he might just get away with it, even now.

"Right," came a posh voice, "we've got a few minutes before we're over the dropping zone. Check your straps and we'll get the gate open. George, you get the packs out."

The packs, thought Ted, as a terrible fear reared up inside him. Of course, that's what was in the boxes; he'd guessed at it earlier and now, it was all so obvious.

Ted began to think frantically how he'd explain, what he'd say, when the plane started juddering violently. Everything inside rattled, the wings creaked like an old tree. Ted didn't know if this was usual. Then, came a high-pitched grating noise and a terrifying bang.

"What the hell," shouted one of the men.

"Christ! The engine! These bloody Whitleys!"

Ted could smell the smoke and taste it too, bitter in his mouth. Suddenly, he remembered the puddle of oil he'd seen earlier beneath the engine. God! He'd been such an idiot. Trails of sweat ran down his cheeks, his heart thumped like it wanted to escape from his chest and his head felt fuzzy. He was struggling for breath, knowing that he had little choice now but to show himself.

Ted didn't have to think about it anymore; the tarpaulin was swung back and a waft of warm air and light fell over him.

"Bleedin' Nora!"

"Jesus!"

"What the devil!"

Six sets of eyes fixed themselves upon him and for a few long seconds the men just stared.

"What the bloody hell are you playing at laddie?" shouted a Scottish voice.

Ted felt a pressure welling up inside him, as his shoulders started to heave. He didn't want to cry, not in front of these men.

He was fourteen and too old for that, but there was no stopping the big wet tears that came rolling down his cheeks.

"I got on..."

Ted couldn't get his words out.

"Never mind how you got on lad. We've gotta get you off and pretty bloody quick too."

The men glared at him, until the man they'd been spying on earlier took over.

"I'll take 'im down with me." He had a familiar accent, a Manchester man, from his neck of the woods.

"That's not possible," said the posh one.

"We've no choice. We've only got six parachutes. Any better ideas?"

The smoke in the cabin was making them cough, as the pilot shouted through from the cockpit, his voice loud and urgent.

"Emergency landing! Bail out."

Everything happened rapidly after that.

Ted watched them open the boxes, from the sides, using keys from their belts. Then, the men bundled out the packs of parachutes and all the other emergency equipment.

"Get your sweater on. This too."

It was the man who was taking him down and he threw an old jacket towards Ted. Then, he passed a spare harness over to a couple of the others who quickly strapped it first around Ted's upper body, then, around the man behind, so they were both facing the same way. Finally, a trap door in the base of the plane was unlatched. It swung open, leaving the cold wind to come blasting in.

Ted stayed silent in the frenetic activity. The blood flowed freely through his arms and legs again and he should have been thankful for the air too, but instead it was making him shiver.

"Right, we're up first."

The man's voice was loud in Ted's ear, as the others helped them sidle awkwardly to the edge of the gaping hole. Finally, they were sitting right on the edge, their legs dangling in the wind. Ted felt like he'd burst.

"I'm George by the way, what's your name?"

Ted didn't answer.

"Well?"

"Ted! It's Ted! I can't jump. I'm scared of heights!" It came hurtling out, like it was going to make a difference.

"Scared of heights! Unbelievable!"

Ted felt George take a long deep breath.

"Well, Ted, this is gonna cure you!"

Ted's body was rigid, every part of it straining to stay where it was. He turned his head to the side and screwed his eyes up, trying to make everything disappear, but it was no use. A cold wall of wind was against him and there was nothing he could do, as he felt himself being tipped forward, over the edge and out into the open sky.

Icy gusts screeched into Ted's ears, howling and biting into him. As they fell, Ted felt just one thing, the rushing, rushing through nothingness, only space and air. It was the strangest thing, because Ted didn't feel he could breathe, not until, without warning came a kind of thud, a fierce jerk and a loud whooshing sound.

Ted opened his eyes and looked skyward for the source of the noise. The parachute was unravelling; a dark shadow streaming into the light, trapping the air in its folds, as it spread itself like a crescent moon in the endless blue. Ted breathed out and looked down.

Everything went silent. The fast pace of events had slowed. It was as if an emergency brake had been pulled and like a snapshot in time, Ted's world stood still. The park stretched beneath him, the lake glittered in the sun and the mansion that had seemed so grand and unreachable looked tiny enough to pick up. Even the towering trees, so invincible to him earlier, looked small now.

The silence vanished, as George shouted into his ear to brace himself. He could hear the struggling engine of the plane too and smell the acrid smoke again, as he watched it crash landing close to the mansion. Out of the corners of his eyes, he saw the sky busy with the other paratroopers all floating down, but right now it was his turn. The pace picked up and the ground raced towards him.

It wasn't a soft landing for Ted. George tried to roll them over, but his feet still hit the ground sharply and with such a force that he cried out in agony. It didn't matter. Ted's heart soared and in those first few moments of relief he felt anything was possible; that his mum would be OK, his dad would get home safely; even winning the war seemed hopeful, as he reached through the long grass to touch solid ground.

Waiting for the Kick-Off

JASON E HILL

JIM STUMBLED DOWN THE GRAND STAIRCASE. His left hand glided over the balustrade savouring the smooth, varnished wood. It reminded him of the handle of the rifle Sergeant Cliffe had thrust into his hand in basic training last year. Jim couldn't remember what Cliffe looked like anymore but he did remember the sergeant copping it from a sniper's round as they left the boats at Normandy. Jim shook the thought away and snatched a memory of himself before the War – before *it* happened. He saw himself as a boy jumping the last three steps of the stairs. He smiled and launched himself off the fourth step…

The young maid, carrying the morning's mail on a silver tray, gasped as Jim crashed into a ceramic umbrella pot at the foot of the stairs. It rebounded and rolled along the mosaic tiles, the noise echoing along the long hallway. It came to rest between the maid's feet.

"Goal," Jim said weakly.

"Let me help you up, Sir."

"I'm fine, Sally," Jim said as he struggled to his feet. "Hurry along now. Cobbs Senior won't want his mail delayed."

"Very good, Sir." She curtsied.

Jim followed her into the cavernous morning room where his

mother and father were seated at opposite sides of a large oak table. A starched, green tablecloth filled with fine silver stretched between them.

Jim flopped into a chair. He saw his father's ruddy face glare at him from over the top of *The Daily Telegraph*; his greying handlebar moustache twitching slightly before he disappeared again behind the broadsheet newspaper. Jim stared at the photograph on the front page that showed crowds in Trafalgar Square celebrating under the headline 'JAPAN SURRENDERS!'

From behind the paper, Mr Cobbs spoke. "It's 11 o'clock. You're late for work."

"And why are you still at home? Cobbs & Sons isn't going to run itself, y'know," Jim said, smiling to himself.

His father lowered his newspaper once more and looked him in the eye.

"You know very well I have a meeting with the Mayor today. Or did you forget, like you forgot to shave yesterday?" His large face went beetroot red but his voice was shaking. "You're a bloody laughing stock. You'll not be in *my* factory with only one side of your face shaved again or *trying* to play football on the shop floor!"

Jim burst out laughing. "Well half a man, half a beard!"

His father snapped his paper back open and began to turn the large pages as if they had done him a personal wrong.

"Jim," his mother said quickly, "what *you* do reflects on your father."

Jim shrugged.

"We received a letter from Robert this morning," his mother continued.

"Oh yes? How is the great Bobby Cobbs?"

"He's settling in – all the first team have lodgings in the same street – but he says the training is harder than in the army."

"He never could train for toffee."

She held out the letter, "Why don't you read it?"

"No thanks. I'll read about him in the papers when he scores a hat-trick at Wembley."

"And I'll be there cheering him on," his father growled from behind the newspaper. "Perhaps you should be less sarcastic about your brother. At least he's going to live up to his potential – unlike you."

"Henry, please…" Jim's mother sighed.

"Well, how long will this go on for?" Mr Cobbs snapped. He folded the paper. "He's a headstrong fool. On Manchester United's books at 13 years of age! Both of 'em! Two brothers! It's unheard of! World at his feet but…" He drew breath. "He couldn't wait to be the hero, to get one up on Robert, could he? And now look at him; sixteen years old and not a hope, not a bloody hope." He stood up, clicked his shiny black shoes together and marched out of the room, passing Sally who was hurriedly collecting plates with her head bowed.

Jim's mother patted his hand. "Give him time."

She followed his father out of the room, leaving Jim among the paintings of stern generals on the wall, the fine silverware and the letter from his brother – Bobby Cobbs, the professional footballer.

It was late afternoon when Jim walked out of the sunshine into the half-light of the Fox and Hounds Pub. He had been sent by his father to deliver a letter to the landlord.

Weaving his way through the groups of men dressed in heavy overalls, he followed the grey smoke hanging off the low ceiling. His blonde hair was in stark contrast to the earthy browns and greys that filled the room. Jim leaned against the bar and tried to catch the landlord's eye.

"You've worked out how to use a razor then," a deep voice

came from his left.

Jim turned to see 'Tiny' Tom Turner, a bear of a man who worked in his father's factory and was an old friend of his brother. He was drinking a frothy pint of beer and reading a local newspaper.

"Hullo Tom," Jim laughed, rubbing his chin. It was stubbly already. He had matured young and always looked older than he was. That's what had made lying to the army so easy.

Jim heard a slurred voice behind him. "Nice of you to grace us with your presence, your lordship."

A man wearing scruffy overalls was grinning at Jim. He did a mock bow and came closer.

"Leave off, McGinty," Tom said.

"Jus' paying my respects to me betters, Tom."

Jim could feel McGinty's breath on his face.

"Big prospect weren't you? I see Bobby ended up signing wi' United. What's your father make of you stumbling round his factory when you should be running round Old Trafford?"

"That's enough." Tom growled.

Jim could feel tears pricking his eyes but he dug his fingernails into his palms so he could focus on that pain instead. McGinty didn't let up.

"Did you want to be a war hero as well as a football hero? You really thought it was a good idea to lie about your age and jump off a boat in France with the real men on bloody D-Day?"

Jim took a deep breath. He knew McGinty just wanted to hurt him to get a reaction but, really, what could the man say to hurt him that his father hadn't already said?

"I was just doing my bit, I guess," Jim said quietly. "I heard you spent the War in the barracks' kitchens in Oldham. Did you kill many Germans with your saucepan?"

D.M.G.

There was a roar of laughter. Jim waited for McGinty to hit him.

McGinty looked down at Jim's feet instead. "Saw you doing keepie-up for bets yesterday. 'Ow much did you win, your lordship?"

"It was just a bit of fun."

"How about a little one-on-one outside? Let a few win their money back?"

Jim felt all eyes on him.

"All right," he gulped.

He squinted as he walked back outside. The pub opened into a narrow, cobbled street and faced the high, stone wall of the church grounds. An angry gust of wind blew his hair across his face. As he gathered the strands, he saw money changing hands.

A battered football was thrown between Jim and McGinty. It bounced once before McGinty controlled it and ran past Jim, knocking him over in the process. McGinty kicked it hard through the beer bottle goalposts.

"One-nil!" McGinty shouted. "Not so clever now are you hop-a-long?"

The crowd laughed and jeered. Jim stood up awkwardly.

The ball was kicked in the air and Jim controlled it with one touch. He then kicked it in a graceful curve between the bottles before McGinty could move an inch. There was another surge of noise from the crowd.

The ball was thrown in the air and once again Jim controlled it first. McGinty charged but Jim sidestepped him. He pulled his right leg back to shoot. Just then, McGinty launched a two-footed tackle into Jim's standing leg.

Jim slammed into the ground feeling leather straps snap against his leg.

He heard a burst of laughter and hissing as his mouth oozed

blood. Tangles of hair clung to his face.

"No point trying to move so fast if yer legs can't keep up, your lordship!" McGinty shouted. He pulled the wooden and metal artificial leg from Jim's trouser leg and threw it beside him.

Jim heard every metallic clank of the leg as it bounced on the cobbles. It came to rest in the gutter, in front of a pair of shiny, black shoes.

The crowd of factory workers fell silent, as Jim's father, Henry Cobbs, slowly walked towards Jim. He bent down to touch the false leg, but drew back and walked away again, along the cobbled street.

Jim felt bile in his throat. He sat up and looked at the leg with its damaged leather straps and the stupid shoe on the end of it.

"You owe me three shillings, Cobbsy."

It was McGinty.

Jim wanted to hit him but, before he could say anything, Tom's deep voice rumbled, "Best follow the others back inside, McGinty, or there'll be another spectacle for people to watch. If you get me meaning."

"*He* took the bet, Tom," McGinty sneered before walking off.

"C'mon son, sit up," Tom said to Jim.

"Get off me, I'm fine," Jim shouted.

"Come on, I'll get your leg."

"Leave the bloody thing! I don't want it and I don't want your help. Let go of me you big oaf, let go, I say!"

Jim shook violently. Tears streaked his face.

"It may be hard for you to hear this, Jim, especially from a big oaf like me," Tom said, as he put his newspaper down, "but your father thought he was going to have two professional footballers as sons and, well, now he's not."

"I know, but he's more upset about my injury than I am."

"Give him time."

The breeze came back down the street, flicked Jim's hair and flapped open Tom's newspaper.

Jim smiled. "I think I'll give him his footballer son if it's so important."

"Eh?" Tom frowned.

"Look at this," Jim pointed at a headline in the newspaper, "'Teams Wanted for Regional Cup'. I'm going to put a team together and see if we can't win it."

Tom did not look impressed.

"You can barely walk yer daft beggar. 'Ow you going to play a proper game, eh?"

Just then, the Cobbs' maid, Sally, walked towards them from the shadow of the churchyard wall.

"Did my mother send you to spy on me?" Jim said.

Sally paused and smiled shyly, "I may be able to help you, Sir."

By December the argument with McGinty was a distant memory. Jim had spent the autumn recruiting players to his team, training them and making sure his parents didn't find out. Sally had proven invaluable to the project. The help she'd promised Jim outside the pub turned out to be as strange as it was unexpected.

One Saturday morning in October, she had convinced Jim and Tom to visit The Empress Ballroom in Moston to see her father, Douglas Griggs, who was a ballroom dancing champion.

Jim still chuckled at the memory of the first time they had watched Douglas twirl around the dance floor.

"What the blinkin' 'eck has this got to do with footy?" Tom had grumbled, under the sparkle of the mirror balls.

It wasn't until Sally introduced her father that everything became clear.

After Jim had told Douglas his story and rolled up his trousers to show him his artificial leg, Sally's father did the same and said, "Snap!"

Douglas told them how he'd lost a leg at The Somme and how he had overcome the wound through dancing. Jim could not believe that anyone with a false leg could move so gracefully.

He was soon travelling to the ballroom three times a week for dancing lessons. Jim didn't know if it was the music, but when he danced he almost forgot about the wood, metal and leather strapped to what remained of his left leg. In the months that followed he found it easier to walk, run and more importantly, kick a football.

In the first round Jim and Tom's new team had been drawn against a team of railway workers from Sale. Jim's team consisted mainly of Cobbs' factory workers who had been sworn to secrecy but they were still two outfield players short, with the game less than a week away. However, the match could still go ahead so long as they had nine players.

"I'm more nervous now, than I was when I saw those German bunkers in Normandy," Jim said to Tom as they walked into the pavilion changing rooms on the morning of the match. "What are we going to do with eight men and a cripple, Tom? Perhaps this was a bad idea."

"Well, I've got you one more player. That makes ten," Tom said.

Sitting there, lacing up his boots, was McGinty. He walked towards Jim with an outstretched hand.

Jim shook it very slowly.

"Listen," McGinty said, "I was being a right git. Tom's had a word with me and...well, I know you didn't join up to be a hero," he grinned, "we'd probably all be speaking German if it weren't for people like you. Sorry, chum."

McGinty cleared his throat, sat back down and started stuffing rolled-up newspaper down his socks.

Surprised, Jim glanced at Tom, who just nodded, looking very pleased with himself.

The referee popped his head into the changing room. "OK chaps, it's time."

"Anything to say, boss?" McGinty asked Tom.

Tom cleared his throat dramatically. "Erm..."

For the first time that morning the changing room was filled with laughter as Tom was jeered at and pelted with socks, bandages and water. Jim tried to laugh but the one-man band in his stomach started playing again. He gulped and glanced down at his false leg.

He was last out of the changing room and shivered as the cold air hit him. It was then that he realised how many people were lining the pitch as spectators – there must have been a hundred or more.

Jim stood motionless on the touchline. "Oh, bloody hell," he said under his breath.

"Don't worry, Jim boy," Tom slapped him on the back, "they're not here to see you!"

"Eh?"

Jim walked towards a large crowd that had gathered. He passed the opposing team who were standing open-mouthed. As he got closer he saw a group of men signing books.

"How did you get Man United to come and watch, Jim?" said the right back, Laurie Vickers.

"United?" Jim gasped.

Sure enough, he recognised famous faces. He saw Johnny Carey, Jack Rowley, Charlie Mitten, all smiling and signing autographs.

"Jim," Tom shouted, "meet our *eleventh* man."

Jim looked and there, standing in the same red and white striped kit that he was wearing, was his brother.

"Bobby!"

Bobby hugged him tightly.

"But... what're you doing? How did you know?"

"Sally wrote to me. Got my address from a letter of Mother's. Told me everything, she did."

Jim's head was spinning. He followed Bobby's gaze and saw Sally standing next to her father, Douglas.

Jim struggled for words, "This is an *amateur* cup. You can't play."

"Actually he can," a Scottish voice said.

Jim turned to see a warm-faced man puffing on a pipe. He shook Jim's hand with an iron grip.

"This daft haggis has refused to sign a professional contract since he found out about this match. He's still an amateur *and* he's lucky he can kick a ball straight. Not many people delay signing for Manchester United."

"He's done what!?" A voice thundered.

Jim turned to see his father and mother. His father was glaring at all three of them with equal fury.

"You must be Robert's father." The Scotsman held out his hand. "I'm Busby, Matt Busby."

Jim watched the colour drain out of his father's face.

"Mr Busby, I beg your pardon, I..." Mr Cobbs stammered.

"It's quite all right, really." Busby took a puff of his pipe.

"You say he hasn't signed a contract yet?" Henry Cobbs turned to his eldest son. "Robert, why? Not for this two-bob game, surely?" Mr Cobbs said.

"No." Bobby stared back at his father. "For Jim."

"Truth is, Mr Cobbs," Busby smiled, "once I found out

about this wee game, I wasn't going to let Robert sign until after it anyway." He took another puff on his pipe. "You have quite a son, Mr Cobbs."

"Why, thank you. We knew Robert would make it one..."

"No, no," Busby cut him off, "I was talking about Jim."

Busby patted Jim on the shoulder. "Have a good game, boy." He put his pipe to his mouth and walked off.

Jim's stomach flipped and he saw his father's face flush. The referee's whistle shrilled to signal both teams to get ready to begin.

Jim rushed into position in the centre circle. He snatched a quick glance across at his father, who managed to mouth, "Good luck," before burying his head in his hands. Jim's mother smiled and then turned to comfort her husband.

The sun broke free of the heavy clouds and bathed the pitch in a warm glow. His artificial foot on the ball, Jim waited for the whistle.

Waited to kick...

off.

The Hangman's Daughter

EMMA GEORGE

IT ALL STARTED WHEN MISS CALLEAR announced we weren't having any Scripture lessons that week. We were going to think about Future Careers.

"Please, Miss." Elsie Graham raised her hand. "I don't need a career, Miss. I'm getting married, soon as I can, Miss."

That's most likely true. Elsie Graham's the prettiest in our class, with big blue eyes and silky-smooth hair. Looks like a china doll. I can't stand her. Thinks she's a cut above, and acts like her folks are some kind of royalty. In fact, her dad owns a pub. The Dog and Partridge, on the Oldham Road.

Anyroad, Miss Callear frowned at Elsie over half-moon spectacles.

"It is 1947," she intoned, "and the world is your oyster. The war is over, and opportunities exist like never before. Widen your horizons, girls. Look beyond husbands, and marriage, and babies. What would you be, if you could be anything?"

That made me stop and think. I'd been about to do what I always did, whenever we talked about Future Careers. Write about being a secretary, or a librarian, or any of those dull-but-worthy jobs that make teachers smile and nod and pass straight to the next person.

On my left, Hazel was writing about being a champion figure skater. On my right, Alice was dreaming about becoming a famous scientist.

What would I be, if I could be anything?

I must've spoken out loud without realising, because Elsie jabbed her pencil into my back. "You'll never be anything, Annie Elks," she hissed, "except a sad, lonesome little creep."

That did it. I narrowed my eyes and glared at her, hard as I could. She tutted and turned away. But I'd swear she turned just a little bit pale.

I dipped my pen into the inkwell and wrote in thick black letters,

I'm Going To Be A Hangman.

I underlined it three times, so it looked like a death sentence.

I can't tell you how good that made me feel. Knowing how proud my dad would be. I didn't write aught else. I just sat, and stared at it, and felt that good feeling deep inside.

It lasted all of five minutes, until Miss Callear made her next announcement.

"Tomorrow," she boomed, "you will formulate your Future Career Plans. And you will each present these to the class."

I sighed and tore the page from my pad.

At the top of the next page I wrote *Librarian.*

I didn't underline it. It didn't deserve it.

After school, when the bus dropped me off, I stood and looked at the outside of our shop.

Norman Elks. Greengrocer.

The sign was faded and the paint was peeling. The window display was the same as always. Half a dozen oranges, arranged in a pyramid. A row of Bramleys and some Victoria plums. In pride of place, a bunch of bananas. All made from wax, of course. No one here's seen a banana in years.

I wondered how it would look if Mam were here. She'd paint it, I'm sure. She'd scrub the step and clean the windows and polish the fruit until it sparkled.

But Mam wasn't here, was she? She went and got herself killed years ago, so long that I could hardly remember her. That left me and Dad alone together. Dad never noticed what the shop looked like. Nor did I, mostly.

The door creaked when I opened it. There were no customers. Dad sat behind the scrubbed wooden counter, resting his chin on his hand.

"All right, Dad?"

Dad jumped. He forced a smile onto his face. "All right, Annie, love. How's school?"

"Same as always." I nodded at the plain brown envelope in his hand. "What's that?"

"Prison Commissioners."

My heart lurched, then fell again at Dad's expression. "Not good news?"

Dad pushed the envelope towards me. "Read it."

Sir,

In reply to your letter of application I am directed by the Prison Commissioners to inform you that it is not proposed at present to add your name to the list of persons qualified to assist at executions...

"I thought I'd done it this time," said Dad. "I honestly thought they'd take me on. They've gone for some other bloke instead. After we worked so hard, too."

NORMAN ELKS
GREENGROCER
22-24

We did. I spent all last night testing him on his table of drops. No one stretches a rope better than Dad. Seeing him there, all hunched and humble, I felt a stab of misery.

"Sorry, Dad," was all I could think to say.

"It's never going to happen, Annie," said Dad. "Is it?"

I didn't believe that. Being a hangman wasn't a job. It was Dad's calling. Had been, since Mam got herself killed. When the judge put the black silk square upon his head, and told Mam's killer he'd be hanged by the neck until he was dead, this huge sense of justice filled Dad's heart.

Killers should pay for what they'd done. And Dad should be the one to make them.

Dad wouldn't bind Mum's killer's hands behind his back, or tighten the strap around his legs. He wouldn't cover his face with a white hood, or place the noose around his neck. But he could do it to others.

My dad, the hangman.

My dad, the avenger.

"That's not true," I said. "Remember how you felt when Mam died. You couldn't be aught else."

Dad looked shrivelled, like a Bramley that's left too long on the shelf. As if every drop of hope had drained out of him.

"Maybe," he said. "Or maybe I just wanted to be someone. Someone who mattered."

"You matter to me," I told him. But I knew that wasn't enough.

In the shed, I squeezed round boxes crammed full of Mam's stuff. Behind them were our makeshift gallows. They weren't life-size, of course. Dad built them when I was small, to show me how hanging worked. We practised on teddies and golliwogs, stringing weights around their necks so we could try out different drops. If I was good, Dad'd find me a rabbit. I'd feel its heart quiver beneath its fur as I placed the noose around its neck. A quick drop, a single snap, and bam.

I find my own rabbits now. I hanged the last one two nights ago. It was crouched in the field at the back of the shop, eyes glazed with misery, leg chewed like a fox'd got it. When its neck snapped, my pain all vanished, quick as you like.

The rabbit's, too.

It still hung there, swaying slightly, head lolling to one side. A good clean break. I stroked its soft pale fur, and a fresh determination filled my heart.

If the Prison Commissioners wouldn't make Dad into a hangman, I'd do it instead.

It shouldn't be difficult. There'd been rumours, for years, that a hangman lived in our town. No one knew who he was. He didn't want anyone to know.

I couldn't understand that. I'd have shouted it from the rooftops.

But it made everything easier for me.

Next day, we sat through presentation after presentation of Future Career Plans. Teachers. Nurses. Even a zookeeper. Elsie Graham swished her hair back and told us she was going to be a film star. Miss Callear looked quite impressed when she said she'd start out in repertory theatre. Then she ruined it by saying she'd marry a hot-shot director with masses of money.

"You might want to consider some alternatives," said Miss Callear through pursed lips. "Annie?"

I stood and took a deep breath. "I'm going to be a hangman," I said.

I could see them all. Hazel's frown. Alice's open mouth. Elsie's complete, absolute amazement.

"A hangman." Miss Callear blinked several times behind her spectacles. "You want to be a hangman."

"You said we should broaden our horizons," I said. "You asked what we'd be, if we could be anything."

"But why on earth –,"

I held up my notepad. "I've written it all down, like you told us, Miss."

"Have you, indeed."

I spoke rapidly, before she could stop me. "Exams. I don't need them. There's a course at Pentonville Prison, in London. They send you there if they like you."

"Who does?" That was Hazel. "Who sends you there?"

"The Prison Commissioners. You write and ask them to consider you. If they think you'll do, they give you an interview."

"Thank-you, Annie," said Miss Callear. "I think that's all –,"

"But I've got more!" I babbled on. "There's not enough hangings for a full-time job. There were twenty four, last year, all told. And that was a good year. So I'll do summut else, that lets me take days off. Keep on Dad's shop, maybe. And I'll have to be good at maths."

"Why?" asked Alice.

"To calculate the drops."

"Drops?" asked Hazel. "What're drops?"

"The length of the rope. It's worked out by how much you weigh. Say you're fourteen stone." That's what Miss Callear was, I reckoned. Her face told me I was right. "Your drop'd be five foot five. But if you're eight stone" – like Elsie – "you'd need a full eight feet."

"Why?" asked Alice. "A rope's a rope, isn't it?"

"Not if you want a quick death. Use the right drop, and your neck breaks like that." I snapped my fingers. "If you don't, you'll hang there for ages, while the rope slowly strangles you. People used to swing on the legs of a hanging man, so death came quicker."

There was a retching sound, and Janet ran from the room, clutching her throat.

"I think we should stop –," Miss Callear began. But I'd no thought of stopping. Nor had anyone else.

"You'd kill people!" Gladys shivered. "How could you?"

I tried to think about Mam, her limbs all twisted, dumped in an alleyway. How her killer was made to pay. But all I could see was the rabbit, the noose tight around its throat. Its soft pale neck broken in two. The good way that made me feel.

Like I could start, all over again.

I blinked, and the rabbit was gone.

"Hangmen don't kill," I said. "They do what the court tells them. They mete out justice. That's what I care about. That's what Dad cares about. Justice."

"Dad?" said Alice. "What's your dad got to do with it?"

That was the question I'd been waiting for.

"Didn't I say?" I said. "My dad's a hangman."

They all stared at me. Best of all was Elsie's expression. She looked stunned, like she'd been smacked in the face by a length of rope.

I stared straight at her.

"My dad's a hangman," I said again. "And I'm going to be one, too."

If I thought everyone would cluster round me at break, I was wrong. They talked about me instead. I knew by the way they stared at me, and whispered behind their hands. And not only the girls in my class. Others, too, all through the school.

I didn't mind. I wanted everyone to know. I bit into my apple, a Cox's Orange Pippin, and thought about what would happen next. Soon the whole town would think Dad was the hangman. People would come into the shop, and shake him by the hand, and wish him well. I didn't think they'd ask straight out. We don't do things like that here. But even if they did, and Dad denied it, no one'd believe him. Everyone knows the hangman shuns publicity.

I closed my eyes, and imagined Dad walking down the street. People looking at him differently. Like he was someone who mattered.

Then maybe, just maybe, he'd start to believe it himself.

The Prison Commissioners might even believe it, too.

Happiness bubbled in my heart.

"Annie?"

I whirled round. Elsie Graham stood right in front of me.

"Why did you say that?" she asked.

"Say what?" I said.

"About your dad being a hangman."

I took another bite from my apple. Its sour-sweet taste lingered on my tongue. "Because it's true."

"Your dad's nothing but a greengrocer. That's why you always stink of cabbages."

"I like cabbages," I said. "Anyroad, you need another job. One that lets you go away. Like I said."

"Then why was the shop still open last week? When Walter Rowland got hanged?"

"Who's Walter Rowland?"

"Don't you know?" scoffed Elsie. "They said he murdered his girlfriend, then dumped her body on a bombsite. He was hanged for it last week."

Dad should've done that. It's exactly the crime he was made to avenge. But Elsie was right. The shop did stay open. I thought quickly.

"There's more than one hangman," I said. "Dad didn't do that one."

"That's strange," said Elsie. "Seeing as he got hanged at Strangeways. Only a couple of miles from here."

How'd she know so much? "They share the work around," I told her. "To make it fair."

"You're lying," said Elsie. "I know you're lying."

I stared daggers at her, right between the eyes. "Prove it."

Elsie opened her mouth, as if to say summut. Then she shook her head, like she'd changed her mind.

"One other thing," she said. "Someone else confessed to that crime. Walter Rowland was innocent."

If Elsie meant to shake me, she didn't. Someone always says a killer didn't do it. But hangmen don't decide guilt or innocence. They carry out orders, best as they can. I folded my arms, and stared at Elsie, till she rolled her eyes and walked away.

No one else talked to me that day. But the next day, girls crept up towards me. First one, then two, then a whole crowd. I'd never been popular before. I'd always been sad Annie, the lonesome creep. Suddenly I had this group of girls, who'd never given me the time of day, hanging on my every word.

I loved it.

I told them everything I knew. What type of rope to use (Italian hemp, thirteen feet long, with chamois leather around the neck). How to tie a noose. Where to position it. And aught I didn't know, like the grittiest details of Dad's old murderers – well, I made it up.

It was easy.

I just told them about Mam, over and over again.

Soon I saw first formers jumping off the schoolyard wall, acting out their own hangings. I saw fifth formers clustered round sheets of paper, working out their own drops. Best of all, I saw Elsie Graham, alone in the schoolyard, refusing to join in. Sometimes she stared daggers at me. I smiled back, gracious in victory.

I said nowt to Dad. But I marvelled at the change in him. Every day, when I came home from school, the shop was filled with customers. Dad wasn't slouched behind the counter. He was weighing out damsons, counting Victorias, and chatting to whoever was there. He hardly looked hunched at all. Instead he stood up, straight as a scaffold.

I didn't go looking for rabbits that week. I didn't need to.

I had that good feeling, all the time.

Friday night, I got home later than usual. I'd gone to a café with a group of fourth formers. The first time anyone'd asked me there. The whole way back, I couldn't stop smiling.

When I got off the bus, I stopped short. The shop was in darkness, the window display nowt but shadows. I couldn't understand it. Dad never closed up till five at the earliest. And it was hardly half past four.

The door opened as usual. I stood on the step, not wanting to enter. "Dad?"

"Annie, love." Dad's voice was more weary than I'd heard in years.

I stepped inside and switched on the light. Dad sat at the counter. He looked more hunched and shrivelled than ever, and his smile was nowt but the tiniest flicker.

"Dad? What's up?"

When Dad said nowt, I locked the door, and switched the shop sign to closed. I went into the kitchen and lit the stove. While I waited for the kettle to boil, thought after thought raced through my mind. Someone'd said summut to him. Someone'd told him what I'd done.

I gripped the table, hard as I could.

Behind me, the kettle hissed and sang.

When I'd wrapped Dad's hands around a mug of sweet tea, I tried again. "What's happened?"

"Sorry, love," said Dad. "I've had a bit of a shock. That's all."

Dad's hands shook, and his tea spilled over. Gently I took the mug from him. "What kind of a shock?"

"This man," said Dad. "He came in the shop. Said he wanted to speak to me."

"Who was he?" I asked.

"He didn't say his name," said Dad. "Though I've seen him around. Anyroad, he shut the shop and sat me down. Said he knew about the Prison Commissioners."

"What about them?" I whispered.

"They were going to consider me. The bloke they took on weren't any good. I was next on their list."

"Dad, that's brilliant!" I leapt up and hugged him. "You're going to be a hangman!"

But Dad was shaking his head. "I would be," he said. "If they hadn't heard rumours."

"What kind of rumours?"

"Rumours that I'd been bragging. He said I'd told everyone I was already a hangman. That puts me straight on their blacklist." Dad looked stunned. "As if I'd do that."

Oh, no. I tried my best not to look guilty. "As if you would."

"Where'd he get that from?" Dad shook his head, all confused.

"Why'd anyone say that?"

I changed the subject, quick. "Who is this man, anyroad?" I asked. "Where d'you know him from?"

"I've seen him in some pub," said Dad. "I think he's the landlord. I did wonder –,"

"What?" I prompted.

"You've heard those rumours, that a hangman lives here? I never believed them. But he knew so much about it, I half-thought it were him."

A horrible suspicion formed in my mind. "What pub was it?" I asked.

Dad frowned. "Let's see. It's out on the Oldham Road. Summut about a dog."

Oh, no. No, no, no. "The Dog and Partridge," I said slowly.

"That's the one," said Dad. "He's got a girl, about your age. Pretty little thing. Annie? You all right, Annie? *Annie?*"

I forced myself to smile, a rictus grin that stretched my lips to breaking. "All right, Dad."

He could never, ever know.

The White Line

IRIS FEINDT

IT ALL STARTED WITH A LINE OF WHITE PAINT on 13th August 1961. Anna watched as the masses of people fled across the line, paint still wet, from East Berlin into West Berlin; to safety. She didn't know what to make of it. She was sure of one thing though: she felt scared.

Anna knew that after the Second World War in 1945, Germany was divided-up into four zones: American, British, French and Soviet. Berlin, which was technically in the Soviet-Zone, was further sliced-up. *Sliced-up like a cake*, Anna thought. She tried to make sense of what she had just seen. *Are they now going to fence us in, so we can't leave? Is the government building a wall around the Eastern-Zone so nobody can get in or out?*

Anna ran home, as fast as she could. She had to tell her sister about this. When she got to her flat on Oderberger Strasse, she called out for Marie.

"Marie, there are people running into West Berlin! I heard them talk about building a wall. A wall!" Anna shouted, catching her breath.

"Your sister isn't here," her step-father said.

"Where is she?" Anna asked.

Her step-father held out a note.

"Read for yourself," he said and walked away into the kitchen. He didn't seem to care. After all, Marie, like Anna, wasn't his child.

This wall will FALL

Anna sat down. She picked up the note.

My dearest Anna and Ulrich,
I'm sorry – I had to leave.
Love,
Marie

Anna's head started to spin. She sobbed. Had her sister run across the line like all those other people? Why had she left her behind?

Anna scuttled to her room, slamming the door. She lay on her bed, filled with gloom. She stared at the ceiling. Her mind started drifting.

She had always felt particularly close to her older sister. Anna's father had died during one of the last bombings of Berlin towards the end of the Second World War. Anna had been only a few weeks old. Marie had been three. Her mother had brought the two of them up alone for several years before marrying their step-father just a year before she had died, too. Sure, Ulrich had tried. But he'd never really felt like family to Anna. Now, she was completely alone. She had no one.

Turning onto her belly, Anna pressed her face into her pillow. She felt something hard and square. Anna reached under the pillow and pulled a book out from underneath it. She looked at it. Her sister had left her something. Just for her: *Animal Farm* by George Orwell. Anna opened the book and saw her sister's handwriting. *Anna! I couldn't find you – I will come and get you. Be patient. Love, Marie.* Anna smiled through the sadness.

A year passed and still there was no sign from Anna's sister. No letter, no postcard, no telegram, no phone call. Just silence.

It was a Tuesday in late September. Anna was walking home from school. Her route took her down Schwedter Strasse, towards the wall. She stopped and looked at the beast of concrete and barbed-wire. *It started out as a line of white paint. Look at it now. It's an actual wall, separating East and West Berlin. Keeping us Eastern Berliners in, like prisoners,* she thought. She looked at the guards, patrolling the wall. Her step-father was one of them. He'd joined shortly after Marie's disappearance. He was guarding the crossing into the West so nobody would escape. *Like Marie did,* Anna thought.

That wasn't what she was taught at school though. *The wall and the guards are here to protect us from the evil that is the West, especially America,* she recited in her head. To Anna that meant: no *Coca-Cola*, no *Monopoly* and worst of all – no Rock 'n' Roll. *Well,* Anna thought, *they don't know I found a way around the no Rock 'n' Roll thing. Pirate Radio!* She smiled to herself and carried on walking.

Anna opened the door to the flat. A few letters that the postman must have delivered earlier were on the floor. She picked up the mail and started walking into the kitchen – she felt peckish. She sat at the kitchen table and flicked through the pile of mail. A postcard with a clover on it caught her eye. She turned the card around. "No stamp," she noticed and looked at the writing. Anna recognised her sister's handwriting instantly.

Enlist a tripe to air do – Hygiene to tow.
Sea gems on sea duty: dim thing.
Rare nag: Mama Far Nil.
Silent to burns me.
Lee Roger Glow.

"But what does it mean?" she said. "It makes no sense." Anna looked at the words again and kept staring until all the letters blurred in front of her eyes. This was when it hit her. *An anagram*, she thought as she heard the front door slam shut. *Ulrich is home.* She quickly put the postcard in her pocket.

"How was school?" he asked.

Anna's step-father was getting ready for the nightshift. He put his uniform on while Anna sat at her desk, pretending to do her homework.

"Don't stay up too late," he said.

Anna looked at him. She had never really felt connected to him.

"Promise," Anna lied. She had big plans while Ulrich was out: working-out the anagram. Part of her felt guilty. Should she tell him about the postcard? But then, he was one of *them* now, preventing people from fleeing East Berlin. No, not telling him was the right decision. It just had to be.

As soon as Anna heard the door close and her step-father's footsteps echo down the two flights of stairs, she got the postcard out, which she had hidden under her mattress.

"Right, let's try and crack this," she said to herself. She started systematically – with the first word, then the second and so on. She wrote down all the different options for each of the words.

"Enlist – Silent/ Listen. A tripe – Pear it/ Pirate. To -- ? Maybe this just means 'to'? Air do – Road I/ Radio. Hygiene to tow – Gone yet Hi? Eighty-one? Tow – Two?"

Adrenaline was pumping through Anna's body and rushing to her head. "I think I got the first bit," she whispered. She didn't want anyone to overhear. "Listen to pirate radio – eighty-one.two. Eighty-one.two? That must be the frequency."

She looked at the next part of the message. Now that she had a vague idea what this was about, it was much easier to decipher the anagram. "*Sea gems on sea duty: dim thing* – Message on Tuesday: midnight." Anna gasped. "It's Tuesday today!" She looked at the clock. It was ten p.m. Had she really been staring at the words for that long? She had to move fast. She looked at the next line: *Rare nag: Mama Far Nil.* "Rare nag? This is a rare nag!"

Anna closed her eyes for a few seconds. The pressure was getting to her. What was her sister trying to tell her? She could understand why it had to be in code – the Stasi checked most mail and if they knew her sister had made contact, they'd try and track her down and arrest her.

"I've got it," Anna said. "Arrange Animal Farm." Anna looked at the next part: *Silent to burns me. Lee Roger Glow.* "Silent is 'listen'. Listen to numbers! But what is Lee Roger Glow? George Orwell!"

Anna sighed. *So Marie wants me to listen to a particular pirate radio station at midnight tonight and she wants me to pay extra attention to the numbers and have Animal Farm ready. Good job Ulrich is working until really late,* Anna thought as she tuned her radio to eighty-one point two. She turned the volume down so the neighbours wouldn't overhear her. She knew she had to be careful. The Stasi had eyes and ears everywhere.

At first, all Anna could hear was white noise. At precisely midnight the white noise stopped and a man's voice became audible. The voice didn't sound familiar.

"One, eight, eleven," he said.

Anna wasted no time and wrote the numbers down.

He continued reading out numbers, in sets of threes, "Three, twenty-two, two. Seventy-eight, fourteen, one. One, two, thirteen. Two, seventeen, five." It was number after number after number. Anna wrote them all down. Then the voice stopped. The white noise returned.

Anna looked at the numbers. "He read them out in sets of threes. Marie told me to have *Animal Farm* ready. So this could be page numbers, line numbers and then the location of the word on the line?" she whispered to herself and opened the novel.

She started flicking through the book, looking for page numbers, counting the lines and the words on each line. She circled each of the words and copied them out. "There is a hole in the hedge," Anna mumbled. "By hedge they must mean wall. There's a hole in the wall?" Her heart was beating so fast that it made her hands shake; in fact, her whole body was shaking now. *A hole in the wall. Freedom. Marie.* She continued deciphering the message. "Meet Clover by Napoleon's grave tonight at one. Be careful." Anna smiled. She knew exactly where she had to go. Her sister was referring to Napoleon Schmidt's grave – their former neighbour. He'd died of old age a few years earlier and Anna still remembered his funeral well. But what if she got caught?

Anna walked through the deserted streets. The streetlights had been switched off, which made it easier to wander the roads unseen. She was breathing heavily as she clutched the postcard and the book in her pockets. If anybody, especially her step-father, knew what she was up to, she'd be in serious trouble. She knew they would lock her up for this. Even worse, they could use the clues to try and track her sister down and then what? Anna couldn't bear thinking of the consequences. She turned around to make sure nobody was following her. She carried on walking until she reached the cemetery.

The cemetery was as quiet as death. Her own footsteps echoed across the ground and she was willing herself to walk more delicately. She manoeuvred through the soft soil of the graveyard until she arrived at Napoleon's grave.

Again, she looked around but her eyes were met by darkness and little else. In the distance, she could hear a church bell strike one a.m. She was on time. But where was Clover? She gazed around. All she could see was a few trees and more graves. She didn't know what to do. "Clover," she whispered. "Clover."

Through the bushes a short distance away, a figure walked through the thick night. Anna felt relief. "Clover," she repeated. As the figure reached her, Anna could see that it was a girl, probably around 20.

"Anna. We have to move fast," she said.

"Where are we going? When will I see my sister?" Anna asked. But there was no time for answers – a policeman was walking up to where the girls stood.

Clover grabbed Anna's hand. "Follow my lead," she whispered. Anna nodded and before she had time to think, the policeman had reached them and shone a torch into their faces. *This is it,* Anna thought. *We've been caught.*

"A bit late for an outing, don't you think?" he said. He sounded smug.

"That all depends," Clover replied.

"Pardon? Have your parents not taught you any manners, young lady?" he said.

"Well, again, that all depends on what you mean by *manners,*" Clover said.

The policeman looked surprised. *What's she playing at?* Anna thought but before she knew it, Clover had taken two steps closer to the policeman and kicked him, with all her force, in the groin. He tumbled to the ground.

"Run," Clover said to Anna, pulling her away from the injured policeman.

The girls ran as fast they could, jumping over graves and through bushes. They could hear him shouting after them but the further they ran, the quieter his voice became. They didn't stop until they reached a house on Bernauer Strasse.

"Quick, get in," Clover commanded and shut the front door to the uninhabited apartment building. Clover took Anna's hand.

"Why are we here?" Anna asked.

"Shush," Clover said and led Anna down a flight of stairs, towards the basement of the building. Once in the basement everything happened very fast.

"Anna, listen to me," Clover started. "There's a tunnel leading into West Berlin, here. Right here. I need you to get into this hole there, and then you have to crawl on all fours through the mud. There's a ladder at the end of the tunnel – you'll see it. Just climb up and your sister will be there, on the other side. She's waiting for you." Clover pushed a large bookcase to the side and removed a rug. She then opened a hatch in the ground.

Anna peered in. It was pitch-black.

"What? I can't get in there! What if it collapses?"Anna said, scared.

"It won't. It's safe." Clover said.

"How long is the tunnel? How long will it take me?"

"Not long." Clover smiled, reassuringly.

"What about you?" Anna asked.

"I'll stay here. There are others who need help."

"But I can't just leave you – you saved me from the policeman. You came to meet me. You've done so much for me and I don't even know you. I don't even know your real name," Anna pleaded.

"It's safer this way. I promise," Clover said. "Now, go!"

And with that, Anna got into the hole. She looked up one last time and saw Clover's face – she looked encouraging. Her face faded away as she closed the hatch, taking the light with her. There was only darkness – never ending darkness. Anna could hear Clover moving the bookcase back to its original position, hiding the hole in the ground.

Anna got on her hands and knees when suddenly, she could hear voices. Clover's voice and... was that the policeman's voice? *How did he find us?* Anna thought, panicking. She didn't dare move a muscle. She held her breath, listening. The sounds were muffled but she could just about make out what they were saying.

"Where is your friend?"

Anna was certain it was the policeman's voice now.

"None of your business," Clover said.

"You tell me where she is right this second or... or I'll have you arrested!"

The muffled conversation was interrupted by one abrupt thump, followed by the sound of someone crashing to the ground.

"Anna, go!" Clover said.

Relieved that Clover was fine, Anna wasted no time. She crawled as fast she could, sensing her way through the tunnel. The space was tight – there was hardly any headroom and all Anna could feel was the mud between her fingers and the damp mingling with her jeans. Her whole body was itchy – soil was getting in through the gaps of her clothes. *Feels like I've been buried alive*, she thought as she continued through the tight space. The smell of earth penetrated her nostrils and she tried her best not to breathe. She tried to make out shapes but it seemed hopeless. She carried on crawling; always hoping Clover wouldn't be found out. *She has to be fine. She has to be.*

Anna had no idea how long she'd been in the tunnel when she saw a faint light in the distance. *The exit.* Gathering all her strength, Anna gave it one last push. The light got closer and closer but it was still dim. She could just about make out the outline of a ladder. *Just like Clover said*, she thought.

Trying to stand up proved more difficult than Anna thought. There was more headroom now, in fact Anna could feel a light breeze on her face, but she had been on all fours for some time and the fear of getting caught had taken its toll. Concentrating, Anna willed herself on, pulling herself up.

It took a few seconds for her eyes to adjust. She took a deep breath. The fresh air felt good as it travelled down to her lungs. Rung by rung she climbed up the ladder into the light. Once out of the tunnel, Anna collapsed. When she opened her eyes, there was her sister, holding her. Anna could feel her sister's tears falling on her mud-stained cheeks.

"Marie," she said.

"Anna – I've missed you."

Key

LIVI MICHAEL

"IN 1605, WHEN THE PLAGUE HIT MANCHESTER, the gates of the town were locked so that no one could escape, and the townspeople were left to die."

"Harsh," I say to Mars Bar, who isn't listening. He's texting someone – holding his phone under the desk.

"Well harsh," I say. Mars Bar ignores me again.

It's our local history project, and usually I wouldn't be listening either, but I've been told I can do the illustrations. Old Crowther probably thought it'd stop me drawing on the desks.

I nudge Mars Bar and he glares at me. "That's harsh, that is," I say.

"What is?"

I roll my eyes. He hasn't heard any of it.

"Locking all them people in to die."

Mars Bar, or James Marsden as he's known to the teachers, stares at me like I'm mad. Probably because I've been listening.

But then he says, "Well – would you want one of them knocking on your door covered in plague boils and pus?"

He has a point. But some of them weren't even ill. I open my mouth to say that, but he glares at me again and goes back to texting.

Meanwhile, Old Crowther's gone on to less interesting stuff

– about the rivers being used for transport. I can feel my brain shutting down, like my computer does sometimes.

Usually it shuts down right at the beginning of class. Especially History. But there's some interesting stuff in this project. About the plague – and the tunnels.

Apparently there's tunnels everywhere under Manchester – you can go from one side of it to the other underground. There used to be a whole other Manchester down there – with streets and shops and that. That's what Crowther says anyway.

Sometimes, when my brain's shutting down, I get really clear pictures in it.

I can see me living in the tunnels – with a gang that does all kinds of stuff – and no one knows where we go to or when we'll appear.

Awesome.

Then I can see the gates closing on all them people. Guards on the other side of the river holding – what? Guns? Swords? Bows and arrows?

All them faces, pressed up against the gates.

Didn't they know about the tunnels? Some of them were built later, of course. And some of them started outside the gates. And – well – they mustn't have known about them – they can't have – or no one'd've been able to shut them in.

Now Old Crowther's holding up a key. Big, black and rusty.

"This might be the actual key used to lock the gates," he said. "In 1605."

No way.

I open the big sketchbook I've been given and start to draw. I draw the key big – so it takes up the whole page.

Then on the next page I start to draw a boy. I don't know who he is. Sometimes I don't know what a thing'll look like until I've drawn it. You'd think it'd be the other way round, but it isn't.

Turns out this boy looks a bit like me – red-brown hair, only not shaved like my hair is – and about my age. He's wearing funny clothes. A kind of tunic and leggings, with straps going up the legs from his sandals.

Mars Bar finishes texting and starts nudging me.

"Give over," I tell him, but he just does it some more. So I tell him again, only I'm not so polite, and he kicks me. And we're just about to start fighting when Old Crowther says, "Sam Heywood, are you listening."

"Yes, actually," I say.

"*Yes, actually,*" says Mars Bar and sniggers. Sometimes he can be a real dork.

I go back to my drawing. I want to draw the boy holding the key. But I don't get very far because Mars Bar gives me a shove and a big line goes straight through my drawing.

I leap up and whack him round the head with my sketchpad. And the next thing I know Old Crowther's bounding towards us.

Course, I'm the one given detention. I have to miss football, which is my best thing. The only things I like in school are football and Art.

I have to sit in this classroom overlooking the sports field and watch them all playing. Even when I look away I can hear them. I hear when Clarksy scores a goal and Skeggsy misses. I hear when Mars Bar's called onto the field instead of me.

Mars Bar's dead when I see him.

They've taken the sketchpad off me, but I've still got my rough book.

I start again with my drawing of the boy, tunic, leggings, sandals. Then I draw myself next to him. We're about the same size, but I'm wearing my favourite hoodie and trainers. And I'm giving him the key.

Funny what comes out when you draw.

On the next page I'm showing him how to get into the tunnel that leads under the river. I draw an entrance to it outside the gates, and steps going down. First I go in then him.

All right – it's not something Crowther'll want for the project – it's just something I'm doing on my own. It's a bit like one of them graphic novels – which are the only books I read.

I don't have time to finish it before detention's over. And I haven't drawn anything for the project yet. I could do it at home, I suppose.

Or I could play on my new computer game – Call of Duty VI.

No contest.

But that night I have a dream.

I'm in the tunnel, under the river. I know I'm under the river because of this sound up above – like the sound you get when you press a shell to your ear, only louder. And there's water coming through – it keeps dripping all around me – drip, drip, drip. My footsteps squelch along the floor – squelch, squelch, squelch. Then there's a sound behind – like footsteps following.

I look round but I can't see anything. Maybe it's an echo. Or more water, dripping through the cracks in the tunnel. The drips sound a bit like footsteps. Or like the ticking of an enormous clock.

That's when I wake up. My head's hanging off the bed, right next to my own clock.

That's what it was, then, I think, relieved.

Never thought I'd be pleased about waking up in time for school.

First time I see him is on the way to the Sports Hall. He's just standing to one side of the corridor as we pass.

New boy, I think, and I don't think much else.

We're playing basketball, five a side, and while I stand with Mars Bar waiting our turn, I see him again.

"Who's that?" I say, nudging Mars Bar.

"Who's what?" he says, but then he's called in. And when I look again I can't see him.

Until I'm just about to strike. I see him then, standing to one side of the pole, just watching.

I almost miss, wobbling in mid-air – but I'm good at throwing and the ball goes in.

I'm not even pleased – or not properly.

"Can't you see him?" I say to Mars Bar.

"See who?" he says back.

"Look!" I tell him, but the new boy's gone.

I'm not happy.

I'm still not happy when we're getting dressed. I stare downwards while I take my trainers off, then fasten the laces of my shoes. I don't want to look up in case I see him again. Because by this time I've worked out what's bothering me.

He's not wearing uniform, this new boy. That's not so strange – sometimes new kids don't have uniform for the first couple of weeks. But he was in the Sports Hall without any kit.

No.

He was wearing a brown tunic and leggings. Sandals with strips of leather crossed up the legs. And his hair –

His hair was the same colour as mine. Only there was more of it, because mine's been shaved.

I don't want to think about it.

When we queue up in the science corridor I keep looking at the boy in front. Skeggsy – or Man Mountain to his friends. I don't look round at all.

But of course, in the science lab, he's there.

"Mars Bar," I say, my voice low with fright. "Can't you see him?"

"Who? Where?"

"The new boy – look!" and I nod my head towards where he stands, saying nothing, doing nothing.

Mars Bar raises his hand.

"Sir – Woody's been sniffing the chemicals again."

I punch him. Hard.

And I don't mention the new boy again, though I can see him right enough. Sometimes in the corner of my eye, sometimes just behind. Still in the same clothes.

Sometimes, when I look at him straight on, he isn't there.

By dinnertime I've had enough. I punch Mars Bar again and tell him to look – properly look. Can't he see the new boy by the side of the prefabs?

"Get stuffed," says Mars Bar, rubbing his arm. And he stalks off with Myers and Skeggsy – his new mates. And they're all making signs around their heads, like I've gone daft.

Maybe I have.

But this time I'm going to do something about it.

I walk straight towards him, keeping my eyes on him all the time in case he disappears.

He doesn't move.

He doesn't do anything.

His face is weird.

There's something odd about his lips, his nose.

Like –

Well –

Like I've drawn them.

But his eyes – they're the strangest. Two dark fingerprints in a face that's as white as a sheet.

Would be, I suppose, if I've drawn it on paper.

His eyes make me want to turn and run.

But I can't run away now, I've got to find out what's going on.

Still, I stop a few paces away. And he's still not moving – just staring with those eyes.

Makes me feel a bit sick.

But I say to him, "What is it?"

"What's going on?"

"What do you want?"

Nothing. Just that look that tugs at me somehow – like there *is* something he wants.

Makes me cross.

Suddenly I'm mad as hell.

"Go away!" I yell at him, waving my arms about.

"Stop following me!"

"I don't want you!"

"Get lost!"

Suddenly there's a scattering of small stones on the wall of the prefab, so I whip round furiously. And there's a little pack of Year 7s on the wall, all laughing at me.

Just because I'm shouting and waving my arms at nothing they can see.

I charge towards them and they run off, still laughing. And of course, by the time I get back, there's no one there.

But he's not gone for good – that'd be too much to hope for. All through Geography I can feel him behind me, sitting at the empty desk.

First I try ignoring him. Then I focus my mind on him without looking his way, and think at him.

What – do – you - want?

Nothing.

Then, when we get to the best lesson of the week, double Art, it happens.

I get my sketchpad back, and I open it up, and there, in old-type writing so that I can hardly read it at first, are the words,

Finish the story

I slap the sketchpad shut, then open it again.

Finish the story

I have to sit down.

"Are you all right, Sam?" Miss Ames says as she walks by. "Will you be doing some work on your Project?"

"Yes Miss, probably," I mumble, still staring at my pad.

But suddenly it's clear to me what I have to do.

Should have thought of it before.

The new boy, or old boy, or whatever he is, has to have somewhere to go. I drew him leaving the town, escaping through a tunnel – but then what? Where could he go?

Who'd want a homeless person that might be carrying the plague?

Old Crowther said that the rich escaped early on – most of them had second homes in the country – but the poor folk didn't have anywhere to go.

The new boy doesn't look rich.

But Crowther also said that most of the townspeople had come to Manchester from the country. So maybe they'd have family there.

Also, there wasn't much of Manchester then – just the area round the cathedral. As soon as you got across the river, you were in woods and open fields.

I pick up my pencils.

After school I set off with my mates as usual. New boy's tagging on behind, but I don't mention him. I'm not getting the tram today. Don't know what he'd make of the tram.

At the main road I split off from my mates saying there's something I have to do. Shopping and stuff. They give me some stick and I ignore them.

Me and New Boy set off past all the shops – Sainsbury's Local, Computer Repairs. Wonder what he makes of them?

When I'm sure my mates can't see me, I take the first turning off the main road, then another, hoping and hoping that this plan is going to work.

And it does work – I can see trees, and grass. We're on a path, through a field.

And there, a little way ahead of us, is The House.

I recognise it right away, of course. Because I drew it. It's a white cottage, standing on its own. Four windows and a fence. Flowers in the garden. I made it as nice as I could.

My heart's banging as I get near, *will it work, will it work,* it bangs.

But there she is, standing in the garden. An older woman, plump and motherly, wearing the kind of clothes I thought she might wear, then.

She's standing by the fence as though she's looking out for us. I'm finding it hard to breathe.

But the new boy breaks away from me and starts to run in a funny, lopsided way (maybe I made one leg longer than the other).

And the woman holds out her arms to him.

"Sam!" she says.

That gives me a funny turn, I can tell you. That's *my* name. But she's saying it again.

"Oh Sam – I didn't think I'd see you again!"

And then I see the sign on the cottage.

I've had enough – I'm off – running as fast as all my football training'll take me. Back towards what I hope is my own house.

First I see some terraced houses, which is good, because they're not from the 17th century. Then there's a street. Then a car.

I've never been so happy to see a street or a car!

I don't stop running till I get to my own street and my own house. I find my key and let myself in, go straight upstairs and fling myself down on my bed.

Heywood's Cottage – that's what the house was called. And he was called Sam.

He couldn't *be* me, that's just daft.

My heart slows down and my brain starts to think.

There's always been Heywoods in this area – that's what my gran says. And one of them's always called Sam.

Her dad was called Sam, and his dad before him.

What if new boy was my great, great, great, great, great granddad, or something?

But how could I have drawn him?

And what if he'd died of the plague?

I can't think any more – I've had enough thinking.

Makes your brain burst, just thinking about it.

The Authors

David Crabtree is a student currently studying Writing for Children at Manchester Metropolitan University. He has lived in Manchester for the last four years after moving out of his home in Derbyshire. David primarily writes teen horror, fantasy and science fiction, but has also dabbled in comedy and historical fiction. He is working on his first novel, a dark fantasy story, and hopes to continue writing in the future.

Jason E Hill lives in Lincolnshire with his wife, two children and a Labrador called Trumpet. He knew he wanted to be a writer after creating a comic, *The Adventures of Super Zest* – a story of good versus evil featuring soap and cleaning products as characters – when he was 9. He's not much more sensible now.

Kat Williams lives in North Wales and is a 2012 graduate of the English degree at Manchester Metropolitan University. She is now pursuing the MA in Creative Writing for Children also at MMU where she is working towards her first children's novel. Her wicked sense of humour makes her a child at heart and she tends to laugh at her own jokes, (well, someone has to.) Kat believes a good dollop of mash never goes amiss and is the proud owner of a bright orange satchel; so bright that on a sunny day, it's blinding.

Just short of being a butcher, a baker and a candlestick maker, **Lucinda Nettleton** has tried her hand at many past-times including gymnastics, knitting and hamster-training but only writing has stood the test of time. Originally from Chorley in Lancashire, Lucinda now lives in Leicestershire with her husband and meddlesome cat. Lucinda's passion for writing arose during her BA (Hons) English degree, which lead her to undertake a MA in Creative Writing for Children at the same university, MMU. Lucinda enjoys writing fantasy based fiction and can often be found with her nose stuck in a book of mythology.

After reading 'The Lord of the Rings' aged seven, **Anna Mainwaring** wrote her first novel; an unenthusiastic response led to a thirty-five year break. After working in banking (a mistake for someone who is number dyslexic) she became a teacher, where she is easily distracted into telling stories to her classes. When not teaching, looking after two daughters or crying over the housework, she can either be found writing in wine bars or walking up hills. She lives in Stockport with her family and a psychotic goldfish.

Guy Vernon loves to write and is working on a number of short stories as well as his first novel. He also writes plays and enjoys nothing more than subjecting his friends to the enforced acting of his annual Christmas costume drama specials. Despite protests they always come back for more. He is currently studying on the MA in Children's Creative Writing.

Paula Warrington was born and raised in Leicester many years ago – though not so long ago as the Victorian age – and she is inspired by the architecture of past times still visible in the city. She writes historical fiction and enjoys imagining what life would have been like in earlier eras – but on the whole prefers living in a world with electricity and running water.

Alison Padley-Woods grew up in Welwyn Garden City. After graduating in English, at Leeds University, she became a Home Interior Stylist and Writer for magazines including Brides, House & Garden and Vogue Australia. Alison now lives in Knutsford, Cheshire and loves walking, especially in Tatton Park. She currently writes freelance features for an online newspaper The Summit, teaches Creative Writing in schools and is studying at Manchester Metropolitan University for a Creative Writing MA following a career break to bring up her three children Ellie, James and Tom.

Jacqueline Goddard lives in West Norfolk as a Yorkshire lass in extended exile. The absence of moorland and hills is made up for by her enjoyment of big skies and the county's beautiful coastline. She is a Methodist minister, teacher and storyteller. She is co-founder of YLabyrinth: a learning facilitator, which uses storytelling and craft skills to inspire people to find their voice. She is studying for a MA in Creative Writing at MMU.

Matt Killeen was born in Birmingham back when trousers were wide and everything was brown. He has had a great many 'careers', most of which seemed like a good idea at the time, before realising he was actually a writer. After attempting to make a living as a multi-award-winning advertising copywriter and largely ignored music journalist, he now writes for the world's best loved toy company and a former Premier League football club. He lives in London married to his soul mate and is father to a teenage son who is rapidly becoming better at everything than he is.

Originally from York, **Kim Hutson** had a brief dalliance with animation in London before going to study literature at York St John University with a particular interest in children's books and gothic fiction and film. She currently works in a Tudor manor house (with obligatory resident ghosts) with a Salford housing estate as its backdrop. She has also worked at a library, theatre, concert promoter, video shop, and several very dull (but enlightening) offices. She has had several poems published in anthologies including York St John's 'The Word' and won the Salford round of the North West 'Flashback Fiction' competition.

Marie Dentan was born a Swiss national, has studied in England and now lives in Paris. She has been a professional modern and jazz dancer, and a wardrobe assistant. She also worked as a secretary, a market shop assistant, and a nurse auxiliary in a maternity ward. She is a mother of three, two boys and a girl, and loves to share with them her passion for dancing. So when they all get into a good boogie, the neighbours have to endure loud stamping above their heads, which happens several times a week.

L. Michael is the author of four novels for adults and eleven for children, which have won various awards including the Faber Prize and a Nestle Award. *The Whispering Road* was Book of the Month in Border's, US, in May 2005. She has also published short stories in various places, including Granta and Penguin anthologies. Her fifth novel for adults, *Succession*, will be published by Penguin books in 2014.

Much to her regret **N. M. Browne** has never been a sorceress, shapechanger, warrior or werewolf. Instead she has written nine fantasy novels, taught creative writing and spent too much time day dreaming. Her books have been nominated for numerous awards including the Carnegie Medal and she very much hopes that the best is yet to come.

Sherry Ashworth is the author of many novels for adults and children alike. Several of her books for teenagers have won or been shortlisted for awards, including *Blinded by the Light* and *Paralysed.* Until very recently, she lectured in Creative Writing at Manchester Metropolitan University. Now she is concentrating on being a grandmother and models herself somewhat on Mrs Rylands in her story. She lives in Manchester with her husband and an elderly cat, and loves reading, writing, travelling and Uncle Joe's Mint Balls.

Emma George studied English Literature at Oxford University. She lives and works in Stoke-on-Trent, the city in which her current writing project, a historical novel for young adults, is set. Emma is a librarian, and spends her working life encouraging children and adults to enjoy reading. An obsessive reader of young adult fiction, Emma is about to complete her MA in Writing for Children.

Iris Feindt is a German living in Manchester which she finds challenging at times because she prefers coffee to tea and enjoys her chips with mayonnaise rather than gravy. Iris has written a children's novel, numerous short stories and co-edited an anthology of short stories for children about animals, *Animal Stew*, which was launched during the 2012 Manchester Children's Books Festival. Iris is a Creative Practitioner and currently works as an Associate Lecturer in Creative Writing at Manchester Metropolitan University. She runs a small press, *Pandril Press*, with six of her fellow MA graduates.

The Illustrators

Stephanie Coathupe is a UK based illustrator. Inspired by her travels, she enjoys journaling and narrative work (particularly to do with food)! Her art incorporates loose, organic brushwork and influences from nature and picture books. She has spent the summer working in America to research her dissertation, and is looking forward to returning home to complete the third year of her Illustration with Animation degree at Manchester School of Art.

Bridget Collin is a final year student at Manchester Metropolitan University, studying Illustration with Animation. She is inspired by the beauty of traditional drawing styles and retains this delicacy in her work, creating playful and contemporary images mainly using drawing inks. Bridget hopes to work as an illustrator, creating drawings that can be enjoyed by both children and adults alike.

Sam Croasdale is inspired by the works of Edward Gorey and Tim Burton and her work often integrates dark humour into the story. She pays close attention to the personality of the character she is designing so that the illustration brings to life the description in the text. Her work is a mixture of detailed pen drawings and painted textures which are then illustrated digitally to create the final image.

Sam is in her final year of a degree in Illustration with Animation at Manchester School of Art.

Sabina Drinceanu is currently studying Illustration in Iassy, Romania, but for one term she had an Erasmus scholarship at Manchester School of Art. Her work is inspired by Norse and Celtic Mythology and her favourite illustrators are Brian Froud and Alan Lee. She enjoys working with watercolours, ink and coloured pencils, but sometimes she paints with acrylic on canvas.

Born and raised in Cheshire, **Harry Fryer** is an Illustration with Animation student who is studying to complete his final year at Manchester School of Art. With strong passions for comic book culture, conceptual illustration and design, the video gaming industry and storytelling, his inspirations from these areas fuel his work. He greatly enjoys a good solid work of fiction, and occasionally writes and illustrates his own tales. Aspiring to freelance in Illustration, he enjoys creating work over a range of different projects and briefs.

Daniel Garrity Acronym loving SWM, 21yo, currently studying Illustration and Animation at Manchester School of Art. Seeking MBA, for possible work NSA. Enjoys recreational drawing in free time and long strolls beside the beach. GSOH (debatable).

Alexandra Healey is currently in her final year at Manchester School of Art studying Illustration with Animation. She hopes to become a children's illustrator, using her mixed media approach to create contemporary and engaging imagery.

Jennifer Quinn is currently studying Illustration and Animation at Manchester School of Art. Realistic topics with precise details are the central focus in her pieces, which are created using pencil and various other mediums. She especially enjoys using watercolour paints to bring her illustrations to life. In the future, after graduating, she aspires to become a freelance illustrator to fulfil her clients' individual artistic needs.

Stephanie Shaw is from York and now lives, works and plays in Manchester where she is studying Illustration with Animation at Manchester School of Art. She employs a variety of processes, such as printmaking, drawing, painting, and live action and hand-drawn animation. She likes to impart a sense of ambiguity and intrigue in her work. Inspired by and interested in psycho-geography, self-publication, the absurd, folk art, Surrealism and Dada, to name a few.

Nabihah Shireen is a third year student currently studying Illustration with Animation at Manchester School of Art. Within her practice, she enjoys using different media ranging from brush and ink to paints, photography, printmaking, book-making, film and animation. She draws inspiration from both historical and contemporary artists such as Alphonse Mucha, Dante Gabriel Rossetti and Lucinda Rodgers. Visit Nabihah's blog at www.beashireen.tumblr.com

Bethany Thompson likes drawing things. She usually uses a pen dipped in ink but is not averse to the odd brush or pencil. She aims to retain a naive aesthetic, and concentrate on ordinary details of the everyday. Bethany is interested in independent publication - she enjoys making her own books, and recently co-founded Counterpoint magazine. Other interests include cycling and cake. Her work can be found at bethanyillustration.tumblr.com

Bethany White is an English creator/illustrator currently based in Manchester. With a deep desire to understand the unknown, Bethany's work is inspired and influenced by magic and mythologies.

Abigail Woodhouse is a Manchester based artist, born and raised in the countryside of Derbyshire. She is currently studying Illustration with Animation at Manchester School of Art and enjoying developing her own personal style.